"Why is it that customers looking at new products or services that would dramatically change their lives or business for the better find it so hard to embrace and adopt them? *The Human Element* cracks the code. It describes the four forces that act against innovation and provides entrepreneurs the insights and tools on how to overcome them. This book is essential reading for any entrepreneur or innovator looking to accelerate adoption of disruptive innovation."

—Steve Blank, Eight-time entrepreneur-turned-educator and originator of the Lean Startup movement

"Too often marketers rely on features, benefits, and promotion as the way to get customers to adopt a new product or service. But as it turns out, this is only half of the marketing formula. *The Human Element* makes a critical contribution to the world of marketing by identifying the four primary Frictions that inhibit consumers' desires to adopt new offers. This book shows readers not only how to forecast these Frictions, but more importantly, how to overcome them. *The Human Element* is a must read for anyone attempting to launch something new."

—Philip Kotler, "The Father of Modern Marketing," Author of over 80 books and Professor Emeritus at the Kellogg School of Management

"An engrossing read on what it takes to open other people's minds. A leading psychologist and a crackerjack entrepreneur team up to demystify the science and practice of convincing people to let go of the status quo. If you've ever been frustrated by people rejecting an innovative idea or refusing a constructive change, this book might just be what you need."

—Adam Grant, #1 *New York Times* bestselling author of *Think Again* and host of the TED podcast WorkLife

"Adoption of your products and services is key to innovation success. Let this book be your guide."
—Alex Osterwalder, Innovation Thought Leader, Bestselling author of *Business Model Generation* and originator of the Business Model Canvas

"What invisible forces slow or stall even our best innovation efforts? Schonthal and Nordgren identify four "Frictions" that get in the way, and then tell us how to overcome them. *The Human Element* is full of insights for designers, innovators, and executives alike."
—Tom Kelley, Three-time, bestselling author of the *Ten Faces of Innovation, The Art of Innovation,* and *Creative Confidence*

"Thank heavens for friction—it makes driving possible. But when traveling on the innovation superhighway, friction is stifling. In *The Human Element*, Nordgren and Schonthal argue that although a bigger engine can promote creativity, friction-reduction is the secret ingredient. This beautiful, elegant book is the essential tour guide for those of us seeking to develop creative and influential ideas."
—Eli Finkel, Bestselling author of the *All or Nothing Marriage* and Professor at Northwesten University

"Innovation often connotes cutting-edge, advanced, or feature-rich. In this book, however, Schonthal and Nordgren make the case that, after all is said and done, innovation is simply about helping people. The authors provide paradigm-shifting frameworks that will help managers and entrepreneurs improve their odds of success."
—Efosa Ojomo, Author of *The Prosperity Paradox: How Innovation Can Lift Nations Out of Poverty* and leader of the Global Prosperity research group at the Clayton Christensen Institute for Disruptive Innovation

"There's always something standing between ourselves and innovation: an overwhelming and very human resistance to change. The insights Loran Nordgren and David Schonthal surface are important reminders of the care and attention designers need to bring a new idea to life and to build our shared future."

—Sandy Speicher, CEO of IDEO

"A revolutionary approach to bringing new ideas to life. Insightful and engaging, this is a must read for anyone who wants to successfully launch a project, a product, or an idea."

—Francesca Gino, Award-winning Harvard Business School professor, innovation expert, and author of *Rebel Talent: Why It Pays to Break the Rules at Work and Life*

"*The Human Element* pulls back the curtain on the psychological forces that stop people from embracing new ideas and adopting new products. Whether you're a creator looking to execute or an executive looking to create, this book is a timely read."

—Daniel H. Pink, Author of *When*, *Drive*, and *To Sell Is Human*

"The ability to elegantly overcome Friction is one of the most crucial skills an innovator can possess. The problem is, most don't know how to do it! *The Human Element* finally reveals why we're all wired to resist new ideas, and provides intuitive tools and methods to ensure that even the most cutting-edge innovations are enthusiastically received."

—Bob Moesta, Author, educator, and originator of the "jobs-to-be-done" approach to innovation and marketing

"Nordgren and Schonthal offer a revolutionary and profound approach to getting new ideas embraced: Don't follow the conventional path of intensifying your persuasion; instead focus on reducing the friction that fuels resistance. The ideas are eye-opening and the writing is eye-pleasing, elegantly combining fascinating examples with scientific insights. The writing itself personifies the very message of *The Human Element*: it is all fuel, no friction."

—Adam Galinsky, Professor at Columbia Business School, co-author of the bestselling book, *Friend & Foe*, and a popular TED speaker

"Friction Theory is a powerful framework for understanding user behavior. A must read for every product designer."

—Andy MacMillan, Founder and CEO of UserTesting

"Contrary to popular belief, innovations rarely succeed because they are chalk-full of features. This book makes a strong case for forever dispelling this view in favor of a laser-like focus on knocking down the barriers that keep customers from beating a pathway to your door. If you want a new way of thinking about these sources of friction—and more importantly, what to do when you encounter them—you should read this book. It will give you a valuable recipe for how to design and introduce innovations that are a good bet for success in the marketplace."

—Christine Mooreman, T. Austin Finch Sr. Professor of Business Administration, Fuqua School of Business, Duke University, Editor-in-Chief, *Journal of Marketing*

"*The Human Element* underscores the crucial role that empathy plays in innovation and change. It's not enough to talk about it, one must internalize it in order to have the impact they desire. David and Loran will show you how."

—Maelle Gavet, Bestselling author of *Trampled by Unicorns* and CEO of TechStars

THE

HUMAN

ELEMENT

**Overcoming the Resistance
That Awaits New Ideas**

THE

HUMAN

ELEMENT

Loran Nordgren | David Schonthal

WILEY

Published by John Wiley & Sons, Inc., Hoboken, New Jersey.
Published simultaneously in Canada.

For general information on our other products and services or for technical support, please contact our Customer Care Department within the United States at (800) 762-2974, outside the United States at (317) 572-3993 or fax (317) 572-4002.

Wiley publishes in a variety of print and electronic formats and by print-on-demand. Some material included with standard print versions of this book may not be included in ebooks or in print-on-demand. If this book refers to media such as a CD or DVD that is not included in the version you purchased, you may download this material at http://booksupport.wiley.com. For more information about Wiley products, visit www.wiley.com.

Library of Congress Cataloging-in-Publication Data is Available:

ISBN 9781119765042 (Hardback)
ISBN 9781119765066 (ePDF)
ISBN 9781119765059 (ePub)

Cover Design and Images: Kyle Fletcher
SKY10034803_061622

To Erin and Allison.

CONTENTS

1 The Law of Attraction

The Battle between Fuel and Friction

When a bullet is fired from a gun, it leaves the barrel moving 1,300 feet per second, breaking the sound barrier. If shot at the ideal trajectory (45 degrees), it can travel for nearly two miles. But a bullet isn't just powerful. It's equally precise. In a steady hand, a bullet will strike its target with pinpoint accuracy, time and again. What enables such a technologically simple device to achieve such extraordinary power and precision?

Most people's answer is gunpowder.

When the trigger on a gun is pulled, a firing pin strikes the bullet, causing the gunpowder inside the bullet to burn. The burning gunpowder produces gas that rapidly expands, creating enormous pressure inside the barrel of the gun. The only way for the gas to escape is to push the bullet out through the end of the barrel.

A bullet needs gunpowder to fly. But gunpowder alone doesn't enable a bullet to achieve such incredible distance, speed, and accuracy. When an object takes flight, be it a bullet, an airplane, or a pitcher's fastball, two opposing forces are at play. There are propelling forces that thrust the object forward (gunpowder, a jet engine, or a pitcher's arm). And there are constraining forces (gravity and wind resistance) that operate against forward progress.

Gunpowder isn't the wrong answer to the question, *What makes a bullet fly?* It's just woefully incomplete. Gunpowder explains why a bullet leaves the barrel with such tremendous force. But the reason a bullet is able to fly with pinpoint precision over a great distance is because a bullet has been optimized to reduce the principal friction operating against it – drag. Drag is the resistance an object encounters as it moves through air. To experience drag for yourself, try putting your hand out the window while driving on the highway.

Drag is the biggest obstacle to a bullet's flight. That's because the faster an object moves, the more drag it encounters. If you add more gunpowder to a bullet, it will leave the barrel with greater speed. But that increased speed also increases the drag pushing back against the bullet. That is why all bullets are rated according to their drag coefficient – the lower the drag coefficient, the better (and more expensive) the bullet.

A bullet reduces drag in two ways. First, the shape is critical. Streamlined objects with pointed ends cut through wind much better than round or blunt-shaped objects. That is why a bullet, an airplane, and a high-speed train all have the same tapered "nose." A bullet also reduces drag through spiral rotation. Guns have grooves inside the barrel that causes the bullet to rotate. Just like throwing a football, the spiraling action helps the bullet cut through the air, making it less susceptible to cross-winds that might blow it off course.

The reason a bullet flies so well is not because gunpowder gives it thrust. It's because a bullet is aerodynamic. It has been constructed to reduce the friction operating against it. A bullet, or rather people's intuition about what makes a bullet fly, is a good metaphor for the principal idea in this book. Our intuition tells us that for an idea to take flight, we need to give it thrust. And that's true. But imagine building an airplane without taking aerodynamics into account and only thinking about the power of the engines. This is precisely what we do when we launch a new idea or initiative. No wonder so few take flight.[1]

The Law of Attraction

How do you get people to embrace a new idea? Most marketers, innovators, executives, activists, or anyone else in the business of creating change, operate on a deep assumption. It's a view of the world so deeply ingrained in our thinking that we rarely see its influence or question its value. It is called *The Law of Attraction*. It is the belief that the best (and perhaps only) way to convince people to embrace a new idea is to heighten the appeal of the idea itself. We instinctively believe that if we add enough value, people will say yes. This reflex leads us down a path of adding features and benefits to the idea or increasing the sizzle of the messaging – all in the hope of propelling people to get on board. We refer to strategies designed to give an idea thrust as *Fuel*. Fuel is what heightens the appeal of an idea and incites our desire to change.

This book argues that people have the wrong intuitions about how to sell new ideas and create change. By focusing on *Fuel* to enhance attraction, innovators neglect the other half of the equation – the *Friction* that works against the change we seek to create. Frictions are the psychological forces that oppose change. Frictions create drag on innovation. And though they are rarely considered, overcoming these Frictions is essential for creating change.

The conventional, Fuel-based approach to innovation is necessary. Without appeal, an idea won't survive. But Fuel alone is insufficient. To create change we must first understand the forces operating against change. While we might not see them, they are there, quietly undermining our efforts to innovate. When we attempt to overcome these forces by adding more Fuel (as our instincts instruct), we inadvertently intensify the very Friction we are trying to overcome.

The Mystery of the Disappearing Customer

One day David got a call from a company in search of help. The company (we'll call it Beach House) is a fast-growing startup that is redefining how furniture is sold. The company has a unique value proposition. It allows customers to create one-of-a-kind, fully custom-ized furniture (primarily sofas) at a price about 75 percent cheaper than other custom-furniture companies.

Beach House has considerable appeal to young, urban-dwelling millennials seeking to buy their first set of "adult" furniture. A big part of the appeal is the ability to fully customize a new sofa. This goes far beyond just selecting fabrics. Every aspect of the sofa – the style, dimensions, material, even the shape of the sofa legs – is selected by the customer. Many of its customers enjoy spending hours on the site or working with a design specialist in the store to create a sofa that is perfect for them. But something mysterious happens right before would-be customers hit the "Order" button: Nothing. They disappear before completing their purchase.

Beach House wanted to know why so many customers never purchase the furniture they spend hours creating. Logical hypotheses might include things like price, time to delivery, or a desire to shop around a bit more before committing. While these explanations are plausible, they aren't the real reason why.

It turns out, the problem had *nothing* to do with the company's appeal. People love Beach House's customer service, high-quality design, and low prices – all of the motivational attributes that *Fuel* a new purchase. Why then did so few people click "Order"? The answer is that there was a Friction that stood in the customer's way, obstruct-ing them from the purchase they desired to make.

For Beach House customers, what stood in the way of their pur-chase of a new sofa – the villain of the story – was (wait for it . . .) the sofa currently in their home! The Friction that blocked their progress was uncertainty about what to do with their old sofa. Will the garbage truck take it? If not, who will take it? Can they carry the sofa out of the house on their own? If not, who will help them? Customers may want a new sofa, but until they figure out what to do with their current sofa, the vast majority won't make the purchase.

In interview after interview, David heard the same story. People said things like: "My partner and I were really excited about the sofa we had designed with Beach House, but we couldn't complete the purchase until my cousin agreed to take our existing sofa." Or "I loved the Beach House sofa I designed, but I had to wait for 'big trash day' in my community to complete the order. Until someone hauled away my old sofa, there was no way I could do it. I can't live with two big sofas in my small house."

If you are Beach House, what would you do with this insight? Adding features to your sofa does not solve the problem. Nor does lowering your price. You solve this problem by removing the Friction. David's recommendation was for Beach House to proactively offer to remove customers' existing furniture and donate it to families in need. As a result of this simple Friction-reducing strategy, Beach House's conversion rate rose significantly.

The Four Frictions

This book explores the four Frictions that operate *against* innovation and change. Like drag on a bullet, the four Frictions push back against the ideas and initiatives we want to bring into the world. When a physical object is set in motion, the value or importance of the object has nothing to do with the Friction it faces. Coating a bullet in gold increases its value but doesn't reduce its drag. Unfortunately for the innovator, the same is true of new ideas. We would like to believe that a winning idea will face less resistance than an idea of lesser value. Alas, this is not so. A great idea might have greater initial thrust, but the value of an idea does nothing to abate the Frictions pushing against it. This is a big reason why so many indisputably good ideas never materialize. The four Frictions are:

1. **Inertia.** The powerful desire to stick with what we know, despite the limitations. Inertia explains why, when attempting to change behavior, you should always give people multiple options, and why, at least when it comes to sports, Americans are socialists and Europeans are capitalists.

2. **Effort.** The energy (real and perceived) needed to make change happen. Effort explains why Beach House customers never clicked "Order," why shore crabs are such picky eaters, and why New Zealand is the best country to start a business.

3. **Emotion.** The unintended negative emotions created by the very change we seek to make. Emotional Friction is the reason why cake mix took 30 years to catch on, why Tinder surpassed Match.com as the go-to dating app, and why managers often strategically put their best employees in the least important roles.

4. **Reactance.** The impulse to resist being changed. Reactance reveals why Americans waged war against seat belts in the 1980s, why strong evidence is often *worse* than no evidence at all, and why manufacturing plants find it so difficult to change practices.

Despite their power and influence, Frictions are difficult to spot and are therefore easily overlooked. The bang of gunpowder can't be ignored. But wind resistance is an invisible force. This is the tricky thing about Frictions. They exert considerable drag on our ideas, but they often go unseen.

INNOVATION HEADWINDS

Inertia

Does the idea represent a radical break or a slight tweak from the staus quo?

Effort

How difficult is it to implement the idea?

THE IDEA

Emotion

Do people feel threatened by the idea?

Reactance

Does the audience feel pressure to change?

Innovation headwinds: The four Frictions.

Consider the following thought experiment: *"Imagine you run a nonprofit that gives social support to children in hospitals. Your organization encourages people to send "hero cards" – letters of support to hospitalized children. Currently, 18 percent of people who are asked to volunteer to write a hero card do so. You want to increase those numbers. How would you do it?"*

When we posed this question to a group of people, two suggestions came up again and again: explain how the cards help children, and pay people for writing hero cards. So we tested these influence intuitions, along with one of our own. One group received quotes from children explaining how much the cards meant to them. Other people were paid a small amount for each card they wrote. And for a final group of people, we simply made it easier to write a hero card by giving them several templates they could use as inspiration.

The first two interventions barely moved the needle (and the psychological nudge backfired). But when we gave people templates, response rates rose by 60 percent. That is, the very thing that was most effective was the influence technique that didn't occur to anybody.

What made the template approach so effective? Does anyone not think supporting sick children is important? Of course not! They weren't resisting because they didn't think it was a worthy cause; they were reluctant to write because they didn't know *what to write*. They struggled with questions like: "What's appropriate? What words should I use? Should the message be happy or should it express sympathy?" That uncertainty is a Friction that defused the tactics designed to Fuel change. But giving people templates removed the Friction and behavior changed.

The Anatomy of Innovation

All new ideas have four basic elements. And each element has a corresponding Friction. The first element is the degree of change the innovation represents. Does the innovation represent a major break from the status quo or is it a slight tweak on what has been done before? This question determines the level of Inertia the innovation will produce. Radical ideas are likely to run into heavy Inertia headwinds because people inherently distrust and reject unfamiliar and untested ideas.

The second element of innovation concerns the cost of implementation. How much physical and mental exertion is required to implement the change? The answer to this question determines the level of Effort the innovation will produce. When buying a new product, what are the number of steps required to complete a purchase? Once purchased, does using the product involve learning a new routine or operating system? For organizational innovation, the implementation demands can often be considerable, as it might require restructuring roles or creating new work schedules. The greater the implementation demands, the greater the Effort.

The third element of innovation concerns the audience's reaction to the intended change. To what extent does the audience feel threatened by the proposed change? The answer determines how much Emotional Friction the innovation will produce. In the hospital card example, people *feared* writing the wrong message. That anxiety prevented them from doing something they intrinsically wanted to do – help children in need.

The fourth element of innovation captures how the innovator goes about creating change. Does the innovator nurture genuine interest in the idea or does the audience feel pressured to change? Pressure to change produces Reactance. When pressure is high, you should expect people to push back against change.

The Intended Audience

This book is for anyone who wants to introduce something new into the world. It can be a new product, a new service, a new strategy, a new movement, a new behavior, or even a fledgling concept that has yet to settle into its final form. Regardless of what the new thing might be, it will – without exception – require people to change in order to adopt it. In this sense, innovation and change are two sides of the same equation. One cannot be successful without the other.

Humans are creatures of habit. Although we have the capacity to change, we don't change easily. Proposing new ideas without designing their integration into the world is innovation half-done. Books on innovation typically focus attention on the idea itself – the features and benefits of the idea that will make or break its success. This book is about the other side of innovation: *The Human Element*. This book explores the resistance that awaits new ideas – often from the very people we wish to help.

A Note about Ethics

Whenever you set out to change people, you have to take seriously the issue of ethics. What is the line between ethical influence and manipulation? First, we should mention that we are not ethics scholars. We do not presume to draw that line for anyone. But we would like to share the two standards we think about when we put these tools into practice. You could adopt these same standards. You could apply more rigorous standards. You could have no standards. That's up to you. These are the two standards we think about in our work.

Is the Strategy Honest or Deceptive?

We believe people should make informed choices and shouldn't be misled. Unfortunately, many of the tactics people use to get people to embrace change are fundamentally misleading. When you get a phone call from a telemarketer, have you noticed that their first name is often the same as yours? This is an increasingly common technique used by both telemarketers and scam artists. And they use it because it works. As we will see in Chapter 4, it works because of the self-similarity principle. People instinctively like things that are similar to themselves. We are more likely to stay on the line with someone who shares our name for that reason. But it's a deceptive practice, and therefore wouldn't meet our standards.

But notice that there is nothing inherently unethical about using the self-similarity principle to get people to embrace innovation. Imagine instead that the telemarketer does some research and discovers that both of you have an interest in common – perhaps you both share the same hobby. A telemarketer strategically bringing up a *genuine* connection meets our ethical standards.

What Is the Intent?

The other standard we consider is whether the intention is to help or harm. We consider innovation unethical if it's for the purpose of personal gain *at the expense of others*. Scam artists have nefarious intent. They seek to enrich themselves at great cost to others. The stories we cover in this book are about people who see a better way to do things and set out to bring that improvement into the world. Some of these stories are about innovators driven principally by altruism. Others are about innovators driven chiefly by profit. Both meet our ethical principles. Our red line is when others are hurt or disadvantaged in the pursuit of that profit. This is a messy and subjective standard. But we believe having an imprecise ethical guidepost is better than having none at all.

2 Thinking in Fuel

The Reasons a Fuel-Based Mindset Rules the World

A car salesperson is expected to sell about 10 cars a month. That's the industry average. The more ambitious aspire to break into the "20-a-month club." A salesperson who sells 30 cars a month can get a job at any dealership in the country.

And then there is Ali Reda.

Ali Reda isn't just the best car salesperson in the world, he single-handedly outsells most dealerships. In 2017, Reda broke a 44-year-old record by moving 1,582 cars off the lots of Les Stanford Chevrolet and Cadillac in Dearborn, Michigan (the national average is just over 1,000 per dealership) – 1,582 cars in one year. That means Ali Reda was selling an average of 132 cars a month, or 4.5 cars per day. And 2017 wasn't a fluke. Ali Reda produces numbers like this month after month, year after year.[1]

How is performance at this level even possible? What could make one person *12 times* better than the average? When you compare the sales approach of Ali Reda to the typical car salesperson, you begin to see the difference.

The Car Sales Experience

Picture yourself standing in a shiny car showroom. You are immediately greeted with a firm handshake and a hearty smile. "What brings
you in today?" the salesperson asks. You explain that your current
lease is about to end, and you're thinking about changing brands.
You mention some of the problems with your current car and list
the features you've got in mind for the next one. The dealer nods her
head furiously and vocalizes a lot of "uh huh's" as she takes in your list
of requirements.

But as you observe yourself in the interaction, you start to wonder if she is *really* listening to you, or simply waiting for you to stop
talking so she can launch into her sales pitch. The first words out of
her mouth confirm your suspicions.

"You've come at just the right time! We've got some fantastic spe-
cials going on right now, and you won't believe how low our financing
rates are. Why don't we hop into this one right here and take if for
a test drive!" (And yes, the absence of a question mark was deliberate.)

As you get into the driver's seat of the SUV the salesperson
is dying to have you drive, you begin to realize that for the next
45–60 minutes, you are not really in the driver's seat at all. You are
now a passenger in an extended sales pitch designed to blow you away
with all of the features and benefits this new car has to offer. The few
questions you are asked seem designed to push you toward a sale.
"Do you think you'll go with the optional third row of seats? What
will your kids think of the bass on these speakers?"

When you finally break free of the dealership, you know you can
count on a relentless chain of automated text messages and emails
from the dealer asking if you are "still interested in that SUV you
drove the other day" and informing you of the new promotions and
offers that have miraculously become available since the last time you
visited – the torturous souvenirs of a trip you never wanted to go on
in the first place.

This might be a dramatized picture of the car-buying experience. But it is true enough (and prevalent enough) that it feels very familiar. And it is this script playing out in our mind that makes us think twice before we set foot in a car dealership.

The Fuel-Based Mindset

In most animal species, it is the female that selects the mate. Reproduction is generally a bigger investment for females than males, so they need to be selective. Females, of course, want to find the best available mate – the fittest, strongest male that will give their offspring the best chance of survival. And males go to incredible lengths to prove they are the best. They puff out their chest, display their antlers, belt-out mating calls, and show off their plumage – all of these signals are designed to convince females that they are the best option around.

Selecting a car works in much the same way. When you decide to buy a car, you set out to find the best car for you. What one wants in a car varies from person to person, but all car buyers are in a quest to find the ideal option for them. Every aspect of the dealership experience is designed to convince you that the cars they offer are the best fit for your needs. All of the features and benefits they demonstrate during the test drive are part of the courtship ritual. They have a short amount of time to share all the golden nuggets of information that might tantalize you into choosing their car. Dealers don't know *which* golden nugget will tip the scale, so they are going to share the whole goldmine with you – just in case.

Although Americans love their cars, they loathe the process of buying them. That's because people fundamentally distrust car dealers. Buying a car, perhaps more than any other major purchase, pits the dealer against the buyer. The assumption buyers make when walking into a dealership is that the dealer intends to talk you into a bad deal. Imagine walking into a car dealership and telling them that you'll accept any of the upgrades, performance packages, and service options the dealer recommends. People would never do that because they are certain they would end up overpaying.

To make matters worse, the decision is shrouded in uncertainty. Dealerships have structured the process so that buying a car isn't one decision. It's a series of consequential choices. Let's start with choosing a model. The base model comes with a 2.0-liter four-cylinder engine with 300 horsepower. But for an additional $7,000 you can bump up to the performance model, which gets you a 2.5-liter engine that puts out 350 horsepower. Then you need to decide on upgrades and feature options. Because you have kids, the dealer recommends you get the "driver assist" system and also recommends the "winter package," which comes with heated seats. Once you work through all of those options, you must then decide on financing and maintenance packages. Do you want to lease or buy? The dealer recommends you sign up for the prepay service plan, because you save $200 on each scheduled checkup . . .

Here's the problem. If you agreed to every option presented to you, you'd probably end up paying a premium for a car stuffed with features you don't need. But if you blindly rejected every option and offer, you'd likely have a few regrets. You believe some of these options are in your interest and some aren't. But you can't tell one from the other. What car buyers really want is to have someone they trust guide them through the process. Buyers want the "cheat codes" for the dozens of consequential decisions they are going to face.

The distrust people feel when buying a car is a significant Emotional Friction. Car dealers don't just neglect this Friction, the culture of persistent sales tactics exacerbates it. It is in this context that we can understand the secret to Ali Reda's extraordinary performance. Ali Reda doesn't focus on Fuel. Ali Reda reduces the Emotional Friction of car buying. For starters, Ali Reda doesn't consider himself a *salesperson*. According to Ali:

I am an Advisor for my customers. I am here to genuinely help them with whatever they need. I am only interested in what is in their best interest. Sometimes this means advising them that a competitor's car is better for them and that they should go down the street to check it out. Other times I tell them to wait a couple of months until interest rates are better or until there is a reduction in price of a certain model. Sometimes I even suggest that they not buy a car at all. The moment I start "selling" is the moment I lose them.

You heard that right. The best salesperson in American history doesn't see himself in the business of sales. He's in the business of building trusted relationships. Establishing trust in an industry rooted in distrust isn't easy. It requires sacrifice and conviction. That's why Ail Reda plays the long game. Ali said, "Sometimes it can take seven or eight years for me to sell a customer a car. I am happy to wait until they are really ready. Most dealers are focused on urgency – not letting someone leave the dealership until they have sold a car. I focus on patience. I might not sell you a car today, but I know that at some point you will be back, and when you are, you will be ready to buy a car from me. At that point I will be happy to 'sell' it to you."

Removing distrust from the car buying experience creates deep loyalty. The reason Ali Reda outsells most dealerships isn't because he has a sales pitch that is 12 times smoother than everyone else. He doesn't hold every major car sales record because he was born with extraordinary charisma. Ali Reda performs at this level because once people work with him, they never want to work with anyone else. And they tell their friends. Each day people walk into the dealership *wanting* to buy a car from Ali because a friend insisted they talk to him before going anywhere else.

The car dealer is all of us. Our deep assumption is that *the* way to sell a new idea is to heighten its appeal. We instinctively believe that if we add enough value, people will say yes. We assume that when people say no, it's because the Fuel was insufficient. It is a belief so deeply ingrained in our thinking that we rarely consider it and would struggle to imagine any other approach to innovation. The Fuel-based mindset explains so much of what we do, from adding countless trivial features to software, to bolting a sixth blade onto a shaving razor. If our audience is not responding to our idea, our instinct tells us to puff out our chest and show off our plumage.

Let's be clear: Fuel is essential to the success of new ideas. Without Fuel there is no motivation to change. But having a compelling idea and a well-crafted message is, in our minds, table stakes. For the sake of this book, we will assume that you, the innovator, have these boxes checked. You have a great idea, but despite your best Efforts, you can't quite figure out why people (your investors, customers, partners, colleagues, etc.) say no.

Before we simply tip our caps to the importance of Fuel and move on to Friction, it is important to understand how and why Fuel works, as well its inherent limitations. This chapter explores the limits of Fuel and why, despite its limitations, a Fuel-based mindset remains the default approach to innovation.

Putting New Ideas into Motion

If you transport yourself back to high school physics for a moment, you might recall Newton's first law – an object at rest stays at rest. No matter how aerodynamic an object might be, it still requires an external force to set it in motion.

In the physical world, the forces that set an object in motion include things like propulsion and gravitational pull. These phenomena generate forward progress and spark momentum. Much in the same way a bullet requires an outside force to set it on its path, so too does an idea.

Fuel is the force that makes an idea more attractive and compelling. Fuel covers everything from the features and benefits of the idea itself to the way that it is communicated to the world. The job of Fuel is to enlighten the intended audience on all of the positive attributes and benefits associated with the "new way." The need for Fuel is so well established that we have built entire industries around generating it (advertising, public relations, and product design, to name a few). Our instinct is to think of Fuel as optimistic or progressive in nature – a tool that highlights an idea's benefits and helps one visualize how it will add value to one's life. There are, however, two distinct types of Fuel, and the jobs that they do for us are different sides of the same coin.

Progressive Fuel

Progressive Fuel is the force that makes an idea more attractive and compelling. Not surprisingly, many of the tactics for generating Progressive Fuel are the very things found in a classic marketer's toolbox:

1. **Product.** All the features and benefits of the idea itself.
2. **Place.** The venue or environment where one might encounter the idea (a boardroom, a car showroom, online, in a book, etc.).
3. **Price.** The creation of incentives, discounts, and limited-time offers.
4. **Promotion.** How awareness for the new idea is generated. This is done via activities such as advertising and informal conversations.

These are the classic "4 Ps" of marketing popularized by the renowned marketing guru (and our Kellogg colleague) Philip Kotler.[2] Since the original 4 Ps were popularized, others have built on them to expand this list (and as a bonus, the alliteration!) The compendium of Ps now includes elements such as:

5. **Packaging.** The form a product is delivered and displayed in (if you have ever seen an "unboxing" video, you'll know that this one is having a moment).

6. **Positioning.** What differentiates an idea from other possible choices.

7. **People.** The people associated with the idea. This could be a spokesperson, the idea's originator, or the people who publicly endorse the cause.

As you read these, you will probably nod your head and agree that the "7 Ps" are a sensible approach to amplifying the value and appeal of an innovation. In the case of car sales, most dealers view their roles as *amplifiers* of Progressive Fuel, believing that sooner or later a customer will arrive at the realization that *this* is the car for them.

Aversive Fuel

Because Fuel is designed to heighten appeal, we tend to associate it with positive elements that sweeten the offering. But Fuel isn't always positive in nature. Fuel can also motivate change by highlighting the risks and costs of inaction. Instead of provoking emotions such as optimism and excitement, *Aversive Fuel* sparks feelings of concern, doubt, and anxiety.

Think about the last time you booked a hotel room online. Our bet is that the hotel's website was quick to alert you to the fact that "only 1 room is still available" at the special price being offered. The anxiety of missing out on the discounted rate may have been enough to push you into booking. In management science this phenomenon is called *loss aversion*, and the influence it has on your perception of desirability can be profound (in Chapter 9, we explain why these nudges often backfire).

Similar to the 7 Ps of *Progressive* Fuel above, there are just as many examples of Aversive Fuel, though they don't come with a catchy alliteration. Some examples of Aversive Fuel include:

- **Fear.** The worry or concern caused by the specter of inaction or making the wrong choice.
- **Loss.** The distress one feels when something they have (or are entitled to) is taken away from them.
- **Risk.** The awareness that trying anything new comes with unknown consequences.
- **Regret.** The anticipation of how one will feel should they make the wrong decision.
- **Impatience.** The desire for *immediate* change.

Aversive Fuel tends to be future-focused. It concerns how we expect our *future-selves* will feel about a decision we make in the present. Aversive Fuel is less about the desire to make the "right choice" and more about the fear of making the "wrong choice." We don't want to be told "I told you so" by others or our inner monologue. As a result, Aversive Fuel tends to be aimed more at provoking action than at amplifying the appeal of the idea.

While Fuel may be necessary for an innovation to take hold, it has critical limitations that suppress Fuel's capacity to create change. Understanding these limitations is the first step to breaking out of a Fuel-based mindset. The remainder of this chapter explores the four limitations of Fuel and why, despite these limitations, Fuel remains our default tactic for creating change.

Bad Is Stronger than Good

A doctor asks, "I have good news and bad news: which do you want to hear first?" What would you say? A majority of people (78 percent in a recent study) pick the bad news.[3] This is because, for the human mind, bad is stronger than good. If you've ever gone through a performance review, you'll know what we are talking about.
One negative comment can instantly wash away all the positive observations that preceded it. Psychologists call this the *negativity bias*. Thousands of social experiments confirm the depressing insight that negative experience has a bigger impact on our lives than positive experience. Consider some evidence.

Let's start with marriage. What ratio of positive to negative interactions do married couples need to succeed? A one-to-one ratio would mean that, to be happy, you simply need to balance the negative with the positive. For every negative comment you need at least one compliment in return. According to marriage research, it turns out the ratio is closer to 5–1. That is, for every negative moment – every small argument or slight – you need five positive moments before you are back in your loved one's good graces. For relationships, negative experiences are five times more powerful than equally positive moments.[4]

The same holds for workplace relationships. A recent study looked at the impact a toxic colleague has on work teams. They examined three kinds of bad-apple employees: "withholders" (people who slack or don't pull their weight), "downers" (people who express frequent pessimism, irritation, and other negative emotions), and "jerks" (people who violate norms of respect). They found that if a team had just one person for any of these three categories, performance dropped by 40 percent. And having star performers in the group wasn't enough to overcome the negative influence of just one bad apple. In the workplace, it is true that a few bad apples spoil the cart.[5]

Negativity also dominates our emotional lives. During the 1970s, a psychologist by the name of Paul Ekman identified six basic emotions that are universally experienced in all human cultures: happiness, sadness, disgust, fear, surprise, and anger. What do you notice? Only one of the basic emotions (happiness) is positive. In every recorded language, there are considerably more ways to describe negative emotional experiences.

Negative emotions also pack a bigger psychological punch. A group of psychologists looked at the effects of everyday good and bad events – getting a compliment from your boss, bad weather, getting stuck in traffic, etc. Not surprisingly, good events had a positive impact on people's mood and negative events brought people down. But the duration of the experiences differed dramatically. Positive events were fleeting. The negative events lingered. In one study, having a good day did not have any noticeable impact on the subsequent day. That is, a good Monday didn't carry over to Tuesday. But negative events had a sustained impact – a bad Monday predicted a gloomy Tuesday. This pattern is so robust that it is considered a "law" of human behavior. Specifically, the *law of hedonic asymmetry* states that "pleasure is always contingent on change and disappears with continuous satisfaction, whereas pain persists under persisting Aversive conditions."[6]

Our bias for bad affects how we see almost everything. We remember negative events more intensely than positive events. We process negative information faster than positive information. People are quick to spot an angry face in a crowd, but are much slower to find a smile. This is because the amygdala, the region of the brain responsible for recognizing facial emotion, devotes considerably more neurons to processing danger. A threatening image can trigger our fight-or-flight response in milliseconds, but positive events produce much slower reactions. You can jump back from a snake much faster than you can jump toward your favorite snack.

Our minds are built this way because it was evolutionarily advantageous. Imagine your favorite meal. If a cockroach scurried across your plate – coming into contact with the food for just a moment – would you still eat it? What if you found a hair in your salad or a fly in your soup? For many, the meal would be rendered inedible. Our animal brain instincts tell us no. That's because many things that kill us (think viruses, mold, bacteria), contaminate anything they touch. Their influence spreads. But the inverse isn't true. What is the positive element that would make a bowl of bugs seem delicious? It doesn't exist, because bad contaminates all that it touches but good does not.

When people hesitate to embrace a new idea, there are two broad explanations. Either the idea lacks appeal (insufficient Fuel), or a Friction is blocking progress. Negativity bias has a clear implication – focus on the Frictions. This shift in mindset can be seen in Bob Sutton's wonderful book, *The No Asshole Rule*, which tackles a problem that plagues many companies: low workplace morale. The conventional response to a disengaged workforce is to – this will sound familiar – add benefits. Crank up the positive in hopes of drowning out the bad. What Sutton proposes instead is fearless intolerance for bad people and bad behavior. The negativity bias leads to the realization that benefits and perks will rarely overcome a toxic culture.

The parallels with innovation are striking. When we sell an idea, our focus is on the benefits the idea offers. We implicitly ask ourselves, "How will we seduce them into saying yes?" And when our message is ignored or outright rejected, our response is to crank up the perks. Fuel is important, of course. But Fuel isn't *the mind's* first priority.

Fuel Is Costly

Fuel can propel an idea and do so powerfully. But there's a catch: Fuel is costly. Two properties of Fuel make it so. Fuel is fleeting, and its impact is proportional to the amount of Fuel that is applied. Let's take Fuel's most common currency, money. Money moves people. And innovators often use it to get people to embrace change. Black Friday – where American shoppers wait in lines for hours to get deeply discounted goods – illustrates the influence of money quite well. But it comes at a cost. Take economic development programs, a practice US cities and states use to attract companies through financial incentives. In 2017, Amazon announced its plan to create HQ2, a second corporate headquarters. To win the bid, Amazon encouraged governments to offer it tax breaks and other incentives. Over 200 cities entered the competition, with a number of contenders offering incentives worth billions of dollars. Before that, the state of Wisconsin had handed more than $4 billion to Taiwanese electronics manufacturer Foxconn. Around the same time, Nevada gave Tesla more than $1 billion to build a battery factory.

Nearly all US cities and states do this to make themselves more attractive to companies. But virtually every study on the economic impact of these initiatives points to the same conclusion: the costs of these programs far outweigh the economic benefits. This is in part because small, fiscally responsible bids simply aren't enough to get companies to uproot and move. It takes huge bids and tax breaks to create change, and those offers rarely pay off.

Like companies, employees respond to money. But like companies, it takes a lot of money to move the needle. One recent study asked the simple question: How much of an increase in base salary does one need to improve performance? For the average employee, it was about 8 percent. Paying anything less than that did nothing. This means that if someone makes $150,000 a year, you need to promise them *at least* a $12,000 bonus to see an uptick in performance. Findings like this led the behavioral economist Uri Gneezy to conclude, when it comes to incentives, "Either pay a lot or don't pay at all."[7]

The thrust Fuel provides tends to be fleeting, which makes it even more costly. Take the Scared Straight program, an initiative with a noble cause – to help teenagers avoid prison life. The program first

began in New Jersey in the 1970s and today has spread throughout
the United States and Canada. The idea is simple: give delinquent
teens a visceral, firsthand look at the realities of prison life by spending the day in prison. The climax of the program occurs when a
group of inmates surround the teens and berate them in an attempt
to "scare them straight."

But does it work? Yes and no. Does the program succeed in scar-
ing the teens? An emphatic yes! The teens are terrified. They tremble
and cry when the inmates confront them. But does this experience
reduce the likelihood they end up in jail? Unfortunately, no. The
Scared Straight program, it turns out, doesn't work at all at reducing
crime. Several well-designed experiments have tested whether being
in the program reduces the likelihood of incarceration. All of these
studies show the same thing: being "scared straight" doesn't keep kids
out of prison. In fact, it's worse than that. These programs generally
do more harm than good. Many studies have shown that the programs *increase* the chance a teen will commit a crime, by an average of
13 percent.[8]

Why doesn't a program like this work? It's not because fear isn't
a powerful form of Fuel. It is. The kids say so themselves. By the end
of their day in jail, they are ready to change their ways. They've seen
the light. The problem is that it doesn't last. Fear, like other motiva-
tors, works in the moment and quickly dissipates. That feeling of fear
doesn't stay with them for very long. Fuel creates temporary compliance. This might be fine in one-shot interactions. But if you want
long-term results, Fuel must be continuously applied.

Fuel Is Self-Evident

Another limitation of Fuel is that many good ideas are self-evident.
The value is there on the surface, for everyone to see. Take the
military. A stint in the military has a number of obvious and

psychologically powerful benefits. The military provides *excitement*. It's a chance to see the world, experience new cultures, and go on daring missions. The military offers *camaraderie*. People describe the service as joining a family. The military is a membership into a lifelong community. People don't just want to be part of a community. They want to be *respected* by that community. And the military immediately gives you that, too. We honor and recognize those who serve. The military also gives *purpose*. People want to see how their lives contribute to something bigger. Patriotism gives you that. And finally, there are big *financial* incentives. Serving in the military is many people's path to college and upward mobility.

Does this description of the many benefits military life has to offer tell you anything you didn't already know? We suspect not. The value proposition of joining the military isn't hidden. Through cultural osmosis, American citizens learn about the benefits and opportunities that come with joining the military.

The US Army relies heavily on TV ads to Fuel recruitment. The ads use powerful imagery to bring all the value of the military to life. One ad opens with a soldier on a daring mission with his Special Forces team (excitement and camaraderie). We then see that same soldier coming home to be honored in his hometown parade (respect and patriotism). Finally, the commercial ends with the now former solider applying the technical skills he learned in the military to a high-paying career.

Two kinds of kids reject this message. The "not-for-mes" and the "yeah-buts." The "not-for-mes" want to experience adventure, respect, and all the other benefits the military provides. These are universal needs. Military life just isn't the way they want those needs satisfied. Maybe the culture just isn't for them. Maybe they can rely on their parents, and not the military, to fund college. No amount of messaging is going to move the "not-for-mes."

And then there are the "yeah-buts." The "yeah-buts" are attracted to all that the military offers. But something holds them back from signing up. This is the key audience the military is trying to reach. They use inspirational TV commercials in hopes of pushing them over the line. It turns out, a lot of kids that *dream of* joining the military never do. A powerful Emotional Friction holds them back. The reason many would-be soldiers never enlist is because . . . they are afraid to tell their mom. They don't know how to start the conversation. They are afraid she will be beyond upset at the thought of her child going off to war. Despite all the value that Fuels the idea of enlisting, many just can't overcome the emotional hurdle. Notice how ineffective these TV spots are for the "yeah-buts." It is telling them what they already know without solving the problem they really have.[9]

Most good ideas have obvious benefits. When people aren't receptive to our message, our instinct is to highlight the benefits or find ways on the margins to sweeten the deal. This approach would make sense if the benefits needed to be discovered, but they usually don't.

Fuel Amplifies Friction

In the physical world, applying force to an object has an opposite and equal effect – it increases Friction. The same is true of ideas. Applying Fuel can, quite unintentionally, amplify resistance to the idea. Consider these two examples.

A former student of ours worked at a large environmental nonprofit. The organization had just brought in a new CEO with bold ambitions. Although he inherited an experienced workforce – many employees had been with the organization for their entire career – he feared many had grown complacent. He wanted his team to "live the mission" and he didn't see that commitment from them. So to boost engagement, he created a bold initiative: the 20-for-20 campaign.

The goal was to raise $20 million in 2020. This was a lofty goal. Their best year ever had been 2017, when they raised a little over $17 million. But much of that was due to a once-in-a-lifetime gift. They had raised just $14 million in 2019, so 20-for-20 was truly ambitious. The CEO kicked off the campaign with a celebration. He spoke about his dedication to the mission. Employees were brought on stage to share their success stories and receive applause and accolades. A retired farmer gave an emotional speech about how, without the help of the nonprofit, the community would have been damaged beyond repair. And then, to close out the celebration, came the big reveal: the CEO challenged them to hit the $20 million mark in the upcoming year. His closing line was reportedly, "I am blessed to work with such an amazing group of people. You have done so much for this cause. But I believe we can all do better. We've seen tonight how our cause matters – there are literally lives on the line. So I ask you all to commit to the 20-in-20 challenge – raising 20 million dollars in the next year. I believe you can do it. I know you can do it." That year, they raised just $12 million, $2 million less than the previous year. And they recorded their highest rate of turnover in memory.

The 20-in-20 challenge was meant to give employees the added Fuel they needed to achieve new fundraising heights. Instead, the initiative created strong Emotional Friction. It backfired, we suspect, because employees didn't believe the goal was realistic. They were trying their very best already. And now they were being asked to do even more with the same amount of resources. The CEO was saying, "I believe in you." But what they heard was, "This guy doesn't think we are trying hard enough." They left the celebration feeling insulted, not energized.

Good nutrition during pregnancy is vital for the lifelong health of babies and mothers. Yet most pregnant women don't get what they need. A significant number of pregnant women are deficient in essential nutrients, like vitamin A, D, and E, as well as calcium and iron.

And most are getting too much of what they don't need. Over 70 percent of expecting mothers have far too much sodium in their diet.

The importance of getting the right nutrients isn't lost on pregnant women. They are reminded constantly. Supplements are one solution. But they aren't a perfect fix. Supplements don't address the problem of getting too much of the unhealthy stuff and they can lead to excess nutrient levels. The real solution is to eat nutrient-rich food.

These problems are biggest in lower-income communities. Unhealthy food tends to be cheap and easy. Building a balanced diet isn't just more expensive, it requires planning and preparing meals at home – a difficult task if you are managing multiple jobs without a lot of support.

In the very early stages of his career, Loran was part of a pilot project designed to promote healthy nutrition during pregnancy. At their checkups, women were given pamphlets with information about the importance of eating right – eat a diet rich in fresh fruits and vegetables and avoid fast food and other easy but unhealthy options.

The pilot was a disaster. Women didn't eat any healthier than before. And worse, their beliefs about the importance of healthful eating changed – in the opposite direction. They thought it was *less* important to have a vegetable-rich diet after exposure to the messages. The pilot program was quickly stopped due to the disappointing results.

Eating healthier during pregnancy is an undeniably good idea that we all should embrace. But the message backfired because of the many powerful forces working against healthful eating. Let's start with the fact that it costs $10 to buy five apples and $1.99 to buy a dozen donuts. And add to that the fact that most of the women who received the pamphlets lived in a *food desert* – a town or neighborhood without a full-service supermarket.

Put yourself in the shoes of a low-income woman. You care about nothing more than the health of your baby (it's a self-evident idea), but economic and social hurdles make it difficult. A doctor telling you to eat healthy does what, exactly? It creates tension in your mind that you want to resolve. For many, the only way to reduce the tension is to push back on the message – to conclude that a healthy diet isn't really that important. After all, a lot of kids in your neighborhood grew up on bad diets and they don't have problems. The 20-in-20 challenge and the nutritional campaign are two examples of the many ways in which applying Fuel to an idea can unintentionally increase resistance to it.

These examples illustrate another important consequence of not accounting for Friction. It isn't just the idea that suffers. The innovator suffers, too. The CEO invested heavily in his vision, and put his reputation on the line, only to watch it fail. What does the CEO learn from this experience? Many learn to lose faith in those around them. They learn the "it's impossible to get anything done around here" mentality. Frictions are usually hidden from plain sight. If we don't understand the forces of resistance, we end up placing the blame on the people and institutions that reject our ideas and not the dark forces that undermine them.

Why We Think in Fuel

Why is Fuel the default mindset? To answer this question, we need to understand how the human mind interprets bad outcomes. Suppose you send your resume to a company and no one gets back to you. Why didn't they respond? Or imagine that a colleague of yours starts taking the parking space that's always been (unofficially) yours. Why would she do that? There are many possible explanations for why bad things happen. Maybe the company wasn't impressed with your resume, or maybe they already filled the position. Maybe your colleague took your parking space because she hates you, or maybe she had no idea it was "yours." The reasons we use to explain bad events determine how we interpret the bad news. In life, like in law, intent matters.

Humans have a funny habit of understanding action as the result of *internal* forces and minimize the role of situational causes. We see action primarily as a function of motivation and intent. For example, less than half of American college students vote in general elections. Why are those numbers so low? Because they are apathetic (an internal attribution), we instinctively think. Psychologists call this mental habit the fundamental attribution error. And it is a nearly unbreakable habit of the mind.

Fuel perfectly maps onto our attributional tendencies. Fuel is designed to stoke motivation and intent. Why aren't people buying your product or proposal? "They must not find it exciting," we imagine. If that's the reason your mind constructs, then the way you change that behavior is to increase excitement. And that's what Fuel does.

Connecting bad events with willful intent is buried deep in our DNA. Early civilizations, for example, believed that the weather was a direct manifestation of the mood of the gods. Happy gods brought weather favorable for crops and angry gods punished misdeeds with drought and floods. In fact, the word "climate" comes from the Greek *klima*, which means inclination.

Across these cultures, elaborate rituals were developed to appease the gods. The rainmaking dance is perhaps the most widely known example. In ancient China, the Wu Shamans performed elaborate ceremonies in times of drought. The shamans would dance for hours inside a ring of intense fire. The falling drops of sweat the dance produced were thought to encourage the gods to send rain.

In these rituals we see the same cause-and-effect thinking we observe today. Why aren't the rains coming? Because the gods aren't happy. How do you persuade the gods to bring rain? You appease them. What they didn't consider is that maybe the gods aren't bringing rain simply because they are busy doing other things.

Strangers to Ourselves

There's another reason we think in Fuel. Fuel is easy to see, and Friction hides below the surface. Let's say you spot a better way to do things, and you want to convince people to change. You will explain the facts – how the idea will benefit them. And if presenting the facts isn't enough, you might turn to motivation. Perhaps you make an emotional appeal or create a financial incentive to get people to embrace change. These are general principles that can be applied to any circumstance. No context or background is necessary. How do you convince kids to enlist in the army? Highlight the appeal and provide financial incentives. How do you get pregnant women to improve their diet? Explain the benefits.

Friction is different. It requires discovery. Think back to the Beach House example in the introduction. Imagine if the punchline to that story – the secret that transformed lookers into buyers – was to pay for referrals. What a letdown that ending would be. But why? Because it is an obvious solution. Anyone could have that insight. What's much harder to see is the Friction that holds people back.

Frictions are difficult to spot because they require empathy. They require that you understand your audience and see the world from their perspective. When you are selling change, it's natural to fixate on the idea. But to understand Friction, you need to shift the spotlight from the *idea* to the *audience*.

Even when you shift your focus, the insights you require aren't always easy to find. We like to say Frictions are twice-buried, because there is another layer you must uncover. People often struggle to share what is actually holding them back. If you ask a customer directly, "What concerns do you have?" they might tell you something. But it likely won't be the *real* concern that is standing in their way.

This is partially because people don't always understand the true reasons why they feel the way they do. And even if they did, they might not possess the language to articulate it clearly. People are, in many ways, strangers to themselves. To understand this idea, we must distinguish between feeling and emotion. Feeling is the felt experience. Emotion is the complex, cognitive engine that determines how we feel.

People know how they feel. They know when they feel happy or sad, for instance. But they struggle to accurately explain why. We recently conducted a simple in-class demonstration of this point. We asked two groups of students to share their feedback on a product idea. In the easy condition, we directly gave them the document they needed to write the feedback. In the ever-so-slightly more difficult condition, they had to click on a link to get to the document, which added no more than a few seconds to the task. For reasons we'll explore in Chapter 5, this had a profound influence on behavior. About 70 percent of people shared feedback in the easy condition, but only about 40 percent gave feedback when they had to click on a link.

We then informally asked them to explain why they said yes or no to our request. The main reason they gave? Their level of interest in the task. Those in the easy group tended to say the task would be more fun than those in the slightly harder group. But it's the same task. Fun had absolutely nothing to do with the differences we observed. The slightly harder group *felt* their reluctance – they knew they didn't want to give feedback – but they didn't understand where it came from.

Discovering Friction requires work and patience. It requires that we not only identify *what* people do, but take the time to understand *why* they do it. Detecting Friction demands that we become more anthropologist than marketer – a role for which few organizations have a department.

From Fuel to Friction

"Put a bird on it!" Fans of the IFC comedy series *Portlandia* will recognize this famous line from an episode where two entrepreneurs decide that the way to make ordinary objects more desirable for sale in retail stores is to simply stencil a bird outline on the item – immediately transforming the ordinary object into hipster art.

The satire beautifully depicts our Fuel-based mindset and its shortcomings. We focus our attention on adding gunpowder instead of reducing drag. The limitations of Fuel call for a new approach to innovation. It demands that we stop thinking in Fuel. The rest of this book explores this new way of thinking.

3 ⇕ Inertia

Why We Stick with What We Know

The hit TV series *Breaking Bad* revolves around two unforgettable characters: Walter White, a high school chemistry teacher who turns his talents to manufacturing crystal meth, and Jessie Pinkman, his hapless former student who acts as his street dealer. Walter "cooks" crystal meth from an old, rusty RV. The RV made sense when they first started. But as their operation turns into a multinational network earning unimaginable profits, Jessie wonders why they still use the RV.

JESSE: "Why do we keep it? Why do we cook out of the world's shittiest RV?"

WALT: "Inertia?"

JESSE: "Yeah, that's right. Inertia."

People are often reluctant to embrace new ideas and possibilities, even when the benefits are obvious and indisputable. That's because the human mind prefers familiarity and stability to uncertainty and change. This design feature goes by different names. Psychologists call it the *status quo bias*. Marketing scholars call it the *familiarity effect*. We, like Walter White, call it Inertia. Inertia captures the idea that the human mind is hardwired to favor the familiar. For the innovator, Inertia is an ever-present Friction because new ideas ask people to embrace the unknown. This chapter explains why and what can be done about it.

Picture yourself shipwrecked and stranded on a deserted island. You are in survival mode. As you search the island for resources, you find two types of fruit trees growing abundantly. One is a banana tree. The fruits are smaller than the ones you buy at the grocery store, but they are unmistakably bananas. The other fruit is something you've never seen before. It has bright, orange-red skin and is covered in spikes. Cutting it open reveals a vibrant green flesh filled with yellow seeds. It has a wet, slimy texture that smells of cucumber. Which one are you going to eat? For a survivalist, the choice is obvious. You go with what you know.

For humans, familiarity breeds liking. We favor the known over the unknown. And that makes sense from an evolutionary perspective. Because things that are familiar have been tried and tested and are thus safer than things that have not. Familiarity means that we have survived contact with it in the past. Our instinctive mind recognizes this, and steers us toward the familiar option.

The instinct to favor the familiar is so fundamental to human perception and judgment that we barely notice it. But it is an operating principle that guides much of our actions. Let's consider the evidence.

Love at Repeated Sight

In the 1970s, a psychologist named Robert Zajonc (pronounced Zi-onk) made an observation about animal behavior. He observed that when animals encounter a new object, their initial reaction is fear and avoidance (this is called *neophobia*). But when the animal encounters that object again, the fear quickly recedes. After sufficient exposure, the animal begins to favor the object over less familiar things. Captive chimpanzees, for instance, will avoid new objects when they are first put into their enclosure. If given a toy they haven't seen before, they become immediately anxious. They keep a close eye on this strange object, but from a distance. After a day or two, that initial caution turns to curiosity. Soon the once-feared toy becomes their favorite distraction.

Zajonc was determined to find out if humans operate in the same way. In one of the more memorable experiments, experimenters identified three college-aged people who were rated to be nearly identical in level of attractiveness (psychologists have ways of measuring such things). Each person attended the same 200-person lecture course. They were instructed to be as anonymous as possible. They didn't talk to other students. They weren't vocal in class. They simply attended the lecture, doing their very best to blend in.

What varied was the number of times each student attended. One person showed up just once. Another attended five lectures. And the third attended all 15 lectures. On the last day of class, the three people were brought to the front of the room and the class privately rated the attractiveness of each person.

The results were clear. The person who attended the most lectures was rated the most attractive and the person who showed up just once was rated the least appealing. Because there was no meaningful interaction, it seemed that mere exposure to the individual was responsible for the increase in attractiveness. He termed this phenomenon the *mere exposure effect*.[1]

A great deal of evidence suggests that the more familiar we are with people, objects, and ideas, the more we like them. Our preference for the familiar is so ingrained, it occurs even when we aren't consciously aware of it. To test this idea, Zajonc's team had people stare at a seemingly blank computer screen. Ten different irregular shapes were flashed onto the screen for 50 milliseconds, which is far too fast for the conscious mind to detect (the conscious mind needs 500 milliseconds or more to "see" an object). In the second phase of the experiment, each of the 10 shapes was paired with a new shape that participants had never seen before. People were then asked two questions: Which of these two shapes have you seen before, and which shape do you prefer?

The participants had no conscious memory of the original objects. At 48 percent accuracy, they were simply guessing. However, the subliminal, one-time exposure had a subtle influence on their preferences: they favored the original images roughly 60 percent of the time.[2]

We Buy What We Know

Inertia is a major reason why advertising is so essential for product adoption. Whether searching the countless options in a supermarket or shopping online, one factor tends to predict our buying habits above all else – brand recognition. We buy what we know.

Take online shopping. If you search for "high thread count sheets" on Google, a vertical list of companies selling bed linens appears. Conventional wisdom suggests that whether your product appears in the coveted "first position" at the top of the page or down near the bottom is the critical factor determining what people will click on and ultimately buy. Search engine optimization (SEO) is largely about making sure your product appears first. But a lot of data doesn't support that belief.

Red C is a marketing agency that does extensive research on how people shop online. It has shown that brand familiarity plays a far greater role in click rate than people realize. It has found that roughly 80 percent of the time, people choose a brand they already know – regardless of where it ranks on the page. Whether we are talking cruise lines or meal delivery subscriptions, people will quickly scroll through the list until they find a familiar brand.

Nothing quite captures our distaste for the unfamiliar like the frequent public hysteria over minute changes to the look and feel of products. Take the story of Tropicana's disastrous logo change. In 2009, legendary ad agency Arnell was hired to redesign the Tropicana logo and label. The aim was to give the brand a more modern look. Gone was the iconic image of the straw-punctured orange. The recognizable color scheme was changed, too. The product itself wasn't any different. It was still Tropicana. The box just looked a little different. But people didn't like it. Within two weeks of the rebrand, Tropicana had lost 20 percent of its revenue. Less than 30 days after launch, it pulled the new design off the shelves and went back to the original label. Not long afterward, Arnell, a three-decades-old company, shut down.

Tropicana isn't alone. Ask Facebook. Every time Facebook changes its layout, there's an outcry from users who demand a return to "the way it used to be." If you straddle the Gen-X and millennial generations, you're probably familiar with the TV series *Felicity*. *Time* magazine hailed the show as one of the 100 best of all time and named Keri Russell's character, Felicity Porter, as one of the best TV characters of all time. Despite the show's critical acclaim, *Felicity* stumbled with fans when Keri Russell cut her trademark curly hair. Fans revolted and ratings crashed. The haircut had such a pop culture impact that it turned Felicity's name into a cautionary tale about the dangers of change. Whenever a TV character's look undergoes a major change, it's referred to as "pulling a Felicity."

When the look of a favorite consumer product or cultural icon changes, it just "doesn't feel right" to its loyal customers. That unease and the resulting uproar it causes often catches companies off guard because the reaction to the change seems much bigger than the change itself.

The Pleasure Machine

Suppose there was a machine that would simulate the perfect life for you. You could have celebrity and wealth. You could live in your dream home, surrounded by the friends of your choosing. But none of it would be real. You would spend your life floating in a tank, electrodes attached to your brain. It would seem perfectly real, and you'd have no idea it was an illusion. Would you plug into the pleasure machine for life?

This famous thought experiment, developed by the philosopher Robert Nozick, is known as the pleasure machine. It pits the desire for pleasure and happiness against the desire to live a true, genuine life. When posed this question, people overwhelming reject it. Pure hedonism might be tempting, but people ultimately favor the ups and downs of a real life over simulated perfection. Or so it seems.

Now consider the reformulation of the famous pleasure machine experiment by psychologist Joshua Greene:

> You wake up in a plain white room. You are seated in a reclining chair with a steel contraption on your head. A woman in a white coat is standing over you. "The year is 2659," she explains. "The life with which you are familiar is an experience machine program selected by you some 40 years ago. We at IEM interrupt our client's program at 10-year intervals to ensure client satisfaction. Our records indicate that at your three previous interruptions you deemed your program satisfactory and chose to continue. As before, if you choose to continue with your program, you will return to your life as you know it with no recollection of this interruption. Your friends, loved ones, and projects will all be there. Of course, you may choose to terminate your program at this point if you are unsatisfied for any reason. Do you intend to continue with your program?"[3]

In this situation, people's preferences flip. The majority of people choose to stay in the machine. The trade-off – simulated pleasure versus realism – is exactly the same. What differs is the status quo. The current state of affairs is known and familiar (and thus favored), whereas alternate possibilities are unknown (and thus avoided).[4]

Our desire to stick with what we know helps to explain why Americans are socialists and Europeans are capitalists – at least when it comes to professional sports. The NFL, the top professional sports league in the United States, has a wealth sharing system that would make a Scandinavian smile. It's a system that, by design, punishes success and rewards failure. The worst-performing teams get to pick the best incoming players, while the best teams choose last. And the highest-earning teams share revenue with the small-market teams.

The picture looks very different in European football (aka soccer) leagues. A small handful of mega-clubs compete for the title each year. In Spain, for example, the league is essentially a two-horse race between Barcelona FC and Real Madrid. This dominance is mostly due to the tremendous financial advantages the mega-clubs enjoy. European football has very few salary-cap rules, which creates a system where the 30 wealthiest clubs take 49 percent of the total revenue of the 679 total clubs. And when teams struggle, they aren't given a boost but are instead relegated to the minor leagues.

Americans like and endorse how their league operates and Europeans do too. If someone tried to abolish the wealth sharing system used in the NFL, American fans would largely oppose it. Just as Europeans would likely resist transforming into an American-style, egalitarian system.

This is odd given the political norms in the United States and Europe. Americans have and support a wealth structure that looks a lot like European Football leagues, and Europe has a tax system that mirrors the wealth distribution of the NFL. But a proposal to adopt European tax brackets would doom any American political candidate. And Europeans would revolt if American labor laws were put into place.

Whether we are in a simulated reality or a wealth distribution system, we tend to favor the system we are in. Not because that system is better but because it is familiar.

How Inertia Kills Innovation

Thomas Kuhn, perhaps the most important figure in the philosophy of science, argued that our avoidance of the unknown is the principal obstacle to human progress. Kuhn famously remarked that "new ideas, however well proven and evident, are implemented only when the generations who consider them new die and are replaced by generations who consider the ideas accepted and old." The German physicist Max Planck put it more succinctly: "New ideas advance one funeral at a time."

The principal problem with Inertia (as the name implies), is that it breeds inaction. And inaction is precisely what the innovator is fighting against. Inertia leads us to choose the familiar over the potentially better but uncertain option. This instinct is a big reason why, as the old saying goes, the "good enough is the enemy of great." This thinking leads to stagnation and the rejection of new ideas.

But inaction isn't the only way Inertia harms innovation. Even when people are willing to break from the status quo, Inertia limits the options we are willing to consider when pursuing opportunities or solving problems. Take investment decisions. Investors tend to favor domestic stocks (often referred to as home bias). Japanese investors, for example, put 80 percent of their money in Japan-listed companies, despite these companies accounting for only 9 percent of world capitalization.[5] At present, the 10 largest companies in the world by market capital come from three countries: China, the United States, and Saudi Arabia. This means that the typical Japanese investor lacks exposure to the world's largest companies.

Our preference for the familiar constrains another kind of investment – our social capital. A good professional network is a diverse professional network. Diversity in terms of experience, worldview, training, and so on, exposes people to new ways of thinking and gives access to knowledge, training, and expertise that no one individual could ever possess. For these reasons, many business professionals see having a diverse network as a gateway to success. When Kellogg MBA and executive MBA students are asked why they joined the program, one of the top reasons they give is the opportunity to build a more diverse professional network.

Yet what people value in the abstract and do in practice are two different things. In one executive MBA program, students enrolled in a "business mixer" for a chance to build relationships with other leaders from a wide range of industries. At the event, each student wore an electronic chip that recorded who they talked to and for how long. In a questionnaire taken before the event, the executives indicated that their primary goal was to meet people from *different* industries. But that's not what they actually did. It turns out, the factor that best predicted who they talked to the most during the event was whether or not they already knew the person. People spent most of their time talking to people they knew already. The second-best predictor was whether they were from the same industry. They wanted to diversify, but in practice, lawyers talked with other lawyers, management consultants connected with other management consultants, etc.

Despite the benefits of diversity, our preference for familiarity leads people to form relationships with individuals who are similar to themselves. It's a phenomena sociologists call *homophily*, or love of sameness. We do this because it's more comfortable. It is easier to trust someone who views the world through the same lens you do.

The instinct to favor the familiar suggests that even when we are open to new ideas, innovators and organizations don't consider all the possible opportunities and solutions, just the familiar ones – those they've tried in the past or fit with the culture.

4 ⬍ Overcoming Inertia

How to Transform a Novel Idea into a Familiar Friend

Inertia is a Friction against innovation and change. Overcoming Inertia is straightforward, at least conceptually. We need to transform the unfamiliar into the familiar. Because as familiarity grows, Friction eases. The aim is to make a new idea feel less like a foreign invader and more like an old friend. This chapter explores two broad approaches for overcoming Inertia, which we call *acclimate the idea* and *make it relative*. When used properly, these techniques can ease resistance to new ideas, and even turn our familiarity bias from a Friction into Fuel.

Acclimate the Idea

New ideas are like beer. The first time you tried beer, did you like the taste? For most people, it's not a pleasant experience. But you get used to it. And after a while, the once unpleasant flavor becomes a comfort at the end of a long day.

But imagine if after the very first time you tried beer, you had to make a binding decision about whether you would ever want to have another one. A lot of people would needlessly reject beer simply because they weren't given time to acclimate. If you were trying to promote beer drinking, it would be a terrible approach.

But this is the precise path many leaders and innovators take. Like beer, new ideas often first leave a bad taste in people's mouth. But as familiarity grows, Friction eases. All too often, the first time we announce a new idea is also the moment we ask people to decide on it. Though it's a common occurrence, it's an equally terrible approach. Instead, we want to allow people to acclimate to new ideas *before* we ask for buy-in. As we saw in the last chapter, familiarity comes from exposure to the new idea. Let's look at five strategies we might use to put this into action.

Strategy #1: Repetition

The mere exposure effect is the finding that contact increases liking. There's a variation of this phenomenon that psychologists call the *illusion of truth* effect. It's the notion that the more we hear a statement, the more likely we are to believe it and endorse it. In a typical experiment, people are given a series of statements that are either true or false. For example, they are asked to judge whether a statement like "A Clydesdale is a type of horse" is true (which it is), or whether a "mastiff is a type of horse" (which is not).

After a break – of minutes, days, or even weeks – people complete the second phase of the experiment. This time, some of the statements are new and some they encountered previously in the first phase. The key finding is that people are more likely to think a statement is true if they have seen it before, regardless of whether the statement is actually true or not, simply because they have previously encountered it. The more times they see the statements, the stronger the effect becomes.[1]

Although the repetition-makes-it-true effect has been demonstrated scientifically only in recent years, influential leaders have understood its power for millennia. In the year 132 BCE, a Roman statesman by the name of Cato the Elder traveled to the city of Carthage. He was sent there by Rome to help negotiate peace between Carthage and the Kingdom of Numidia. Upon entering the gates, Cato was shocked by the growing wealth and military power he saw there. A strong Carthage, he feared, was a threat to Rome.

Cato believed that Rome should attack before the great Punic city became too strong. In the Senate, he constantly demanded a war against the Punic city-state. He would end every speech – no matter the topic – with the line "Carthage must be destroyed," knowing that repetition would gradually lead to agreement.

Some 2,000 years later, Napoleon would arrive at this same insight. He remarked that "there is only one figure in rhetoric of serious importance – repetition. A repeated affirmation fixes itself in the mind in such a way that it is accepted in the end as a demonstrated truth."

Repeated exposure makes the novel idea familiar. In politics, this is a bread-and-butter campaign tactic. Say the message enough and voters will start to believe in it. For products, advertising is the conventional way we create repeated exposure. But inside companies, repetition is often a missed opportunity. In our experience, leaders often conceal their ideas – wanting to perfect the details first – until they are ready to launch. This doesn't give employees time and opportunity to acclimate to the new initiative.

Instead, leaders should take a page from Cato the Elder and make sure the idea is featured at every opportunity. In management consulting, this is sometimes called *seeding* the idea. The goal is to plant the idea in people's minds long before they are asked to commit to change. As one Dutch change consultant we interviewed put it, "Tulips bloom in spring but are planted in the fall."

Keep in mind that repetition doesn't have to come from the innovator. If the idea grabs attention, the audience will repeat the idea in their own minds as they "mull it over." Time is a critical element here. It gives the audience the opportunity to become familiar with the idea on their own. Loran conducted a simple in-class experiment to demonstrate this point. He proposed pushing back the due date for an assignment, which would give students more time to complete the assignment but would also mean they had to wait longer to receive their final grade. In his Tuesday evening course, he proposed the change at the end of the lecture and then immediately asked the students to vote. Roughly 30 percent of students voted against the new idea. In his Wednesday evening course, he made the proposal at the beginning of the lecture and then told them they would vote at the end of class, three hours later. Only 5 percent of students objected to the new idea when they had additional time.

Strategy #2: Start Small

New ideas vary in the scope of change they require. Some require only incremental adjustment, while others call for substantial disruption. When a significant change is required, initial exposure is often easier to take when given in small doses. Although people acquire the taste for alcohol over time, many of us have a certain alcohol that we can't stomach (for David, it is Southern Comfort). Invariably, it's because they had way too much the first time they tried it.

The concept of *starting small* is the basis for what is far and away the most effective treatment for phobias. It's called incremental exposure therapy. It works like this. Picture someone with a clinical fear of snakes. This isn't your garden-variety snake aversion. The fear is paralyzing. It's a fear so strong that the person can't even walk in the yard for fear a snake might be hiding in the grass. Now imagine there's a way to overcome that fear – not with a few years or months of therapy, but in just a few hours. Perhaps no more than 45 minutes. That's the promise of incremental exposure therapy.

Therapy begins by having the patient watch through a one-way mirror into another room where a snake is in a glass cage. The sight of the snake is frightening at first, but after 10–15 minutes, the patient gets used to it. That's step one. The therapist might then ask the patient to stand in the doorway of the room containing the snake until this too becomes comfortable. That's step two. For step three, the therapist might have the patient sit in a chair 10 feet from the snake. These gradual steps continue until the patient is sitting with the snake in her lap, often admiring its beauty.

Imagine if the therapist began the session by asking the patient to hold the snake. It would never work. When change feels daunting, people fight against it. The psychology is universal. It doesn't matter whether we are talking about changing personal phobias, consumer buying habits, or organizational practices. Radical change is more likely to succeed if it begins with small steps.

Public Digital is a UK-based consulting firm that helps governments and large institutions transition into the new digital era of business. They work with institutions like the nation of Madagascar to make public services (such as how utilities are paid) faster, more efficient, and more accessible to its citizens. The industry term for this type of organizational evolution is often called *digital transformation*.

Overhauling systems and technologies that have been in place for decades (along with the people who oversee them) creates significant Friction. It is easy for leadership to embrace the prospect of modernization. But front-line workers tend to see things differently. These are people who have spent the better part of their careers delivering products and services in a certain way. And now they are expected to change the way they work overnight.

How does a firm like Public Digital get historic institutions to modernize? Its secret is to *start small.* According to James Stewart, a partner at Public Digital and the firm's chief technology officer, organizations often assume that large change should begin at large scale, when in fact the opposite is true. That's why James avoids the term *digital transformation* in early conversations. *Transformation* implies sweeping change. Instead, Stewart suggests shrinking the scope of the objective. "Rather than asking the organization about their goals for 'digital transformation,' we ask them only about the next important thing that they would like to accomplish. We then use that smaller project as an opportunity to demonstrate the value of taking a new, digital-first approach. It shrinks the size of the challenge to something more palatable. And when it is successful, it provides a beacon for the organization to look to for inspiration."

Public Digital starts small in another way. Instead of trying to indoctrinate an entire institution into embracing modernization all at once, they start by forming one small team – a handful of five to six individuals who are willing to try working in a new way. These "early adopters" then share their experiences with the larger organization. This incremental approach gives the more skeptical members of the organization time to acclimate to the new way.

Repetition is another important tactic Public Digital uses to fight Inertia. They repeat the message by frequently sharing small success stories. For example, when Public Digital was hired to help the state of California IT department modernize, one of the keys to success was, of all things, a blog. According to James,

The team created a simple weekly blog entitled "Doing and Done." Its format was straight forward. The team would share what it was aiming to accomplish in the week ahead and what it had accomplished the week prior. That's it. But they made it available to anyone who was interested. By demystifying the process of transformation and digital service development through the sharing of these micro-moments, the team was able to recruit others to try it themselves. As it turns out, just talking openly about these small bits of progress was as big of an innovation for the California government's transformation effort as the technology itself.

Repetition and starting small are two ways we can transform the familiar into the unfamiliar. Both require time and opportunity, which isn't always available to us. Here are a few other strategies for taming Inertia.

Strategy #3: Find a Familiar Face

Although the message we are selling might be unfamiliar, the messenger doesn't have to be. We are heavily influenced by who communicates information. People are more likely to listen to a message when it comes from someone they know or someone who is similar to themselves.

Rick van Baaren, a psychologist at Nijmegen University in the Netherlands, conducted an experiment in which people were asked to give feedback on a series of ads. That was the ostensible purpose of the experiment. In reality, the experimenter who conducted the study subtly mimicked participants during the interaction. The experimenter would roughly mimic the participant's posture, position of their arms and legs, energy level, and vocal tone, taking care not to be too obvious about it. Psychologists call this mirroring. In a control condition, the experiment was the same except no mirroring occurred.

During the interaction, the experimenter would drop a bunch of pens on the floor, making it look like an accident. Participants who had been mimicked were roughly three times more likely to help pick up the pens. Being mirrored created a feeling of connection that increased goodwill toward the researcher within minutes.[2]

In sales and public speaking, this is called *audience tuning*. A skilled presenter knows how to dial-up the seriousness for a formal audience, but dial it down for a casual crowd. Ali Reda, the world record–setting salesperson we met in Chapter 1, shared an interesting story with us about audience tuning. Ali realized that there was a segment of the car sales market he wasn't reaching – the Mexican American population that was quickly growing in Michigan. Ali felt he didn't understand the needs and interests of this community. That, along with his poor Spanish, were big barriers to building the trust his person-centered sales approach relies on. So when Ali decided to take on a protégé, he brought on Carlos. Carlos had no sales experience but was a member of the Mexican American community in Michigan. Ali proudly reports that Carlos is selling around 30 cars a month, a track record that would land him a job at any dealership in the country. Best of all, Carlos's success hasn't cut into Ali's sales. Carlos has expanded the pie by tapping into a new market.

Strategy #4: Make It Prototypical

Both a robin and an emu are birds. But a robin is a highly prototypical bird. When you think of a bird, you think of something that looks a lot like a robin. An emu is also a bird, but it's an edge case. It fights against the typical image of a bird. Most new ideas, whether it is an innovative product or a new work procedure, belong to a broader category. Ideas that fit the prototype are generally more familiar (and thus better liked) than those that don't. When a new idea doesn't fit the prototype, it causes Friction. The brain has to work harder to understand it. On paper, radical change can sound great because we admire the ambition. But if we pitch an "emu" innovation, a lot of people will struggle with the unfamiliar concept.

Tesla strikes us as a good example of getting it right. When Tesla first launched, the prospect of moving from gas to electric was already a significant change for a lot of people. For a forward-thinking company like Tesla, you might expect them to completely redesign every feature of the car. But the first Tesla to go into production, the Model S, looks like a prototypical car. You know it operates differently and has a bunch of cool new features on the inside, but the look of it is familiar to the eye. Subsequent models, like the falcon-wing doors on the model X or the futuristic design of the cyber truck, are less prototypical. But now that Tesla is an established brand (i.e., the messenger is familiar), they have more room to deviate from the norm.

Strategy #5: Use Analogies

"It's like Uber for dog owners." "It's like a Roomba for your yard." If people aren't familiar with an innovation firsthand, compare it to something they are familiar with. This is called *analogous comparison*. An analogy is simply a comparison that suggests parallels between two things. Analogies work because they make the unfamiliar seem familiar. They help people navigate new territory by making it resemble territory they already know.

John Pollack, a former presidential speechwriter, has written about the power of analogies in his book, *Shortcut: How Analogies Reveal Connections, Spark Innovation, and Sell Our Greatest Ideas.* *Shortcut* shares the story of how in the early days of personal computing, Steve Jobs used analogy to get people to embrace this new technology. Before computers, people worked in a physical world. We used paper and pens and physical file folders and so on. The idea of working in a virtual world was radically different. Or at least *seemed* radically different. What Jobs understood was that a physical office was fundamentally similar to a virtual office. To win over the masses, Jobs drew strong analogies between the traditional workplace people knew well with the new, unfamiliar virtual workplace.

In the pre-computer workplace, when ideas were written on paper it was called . . . a document. When those documents needed to be stored they were put in . . . a folder. And those folders were kept on . . . a desk. Documents, folders, and desktops are the terms we use in our virtual work because Steve Jobs understood that using familiar terms would make the new technology easier to understand. The parallels between the physical and virtual workplace now seem obvious. But in the 1980s, they weren't. Steve Jobs's analogical instinct helped move us into the age of personal computing.

Make It Relative

Picture yourself in downtown Chicago on a beautiful summer day. You wander into the Nike Store. You find a great new pair of shoes for yourself and some workout gear for your kids. The bill: $300. Before you pay, the cashier makes an unexpected offer. The cashier tells you about a Nike discount store that recently opened, just five blocks away. And you are in luck. The same items you intend to purchase are available there. The $300 purchase you're about to make: if you buy it at the discount store, you would save $50. How would that offer make you feel? We bet you'd be thrilled. Or pleasantly surprised, at the very least. And we suspect a great many of you would walk the five blocks.

Now let's consider a parallel example. You are shopping for a new car. You find the car you want. You are ready to put pen-to-paper, when the salesperson makes an unexpected offer. She informs you that there is another showroom about five minutes down the road. The $30,000 car you are about to purchase – if you buy it at the other showroom, you would save $50. Now how would that make you feel? Maybe you'd be offended, underwhelmed, or confused. But you certainly wouldn't be delighted.

Here's the puzzling thing. A rational being would value these offers equally. For roughly the same amount of effort, you are saving the same amount of money – $50. Fifty bucks is fifty bucks. You can have a solid night at a dive bar on $50. But humans aren't rational animals.

What this example reveals is the power of *relativity*. We understand the world entirely – completely – in relative terms. Think about your personality, for a moment. Answer the following questions. On a scale of 1–5, how funny are you? How creative? How ambitious? You might not be consciously aware of it, but you just answered a slightly different question. The question you really asked yourself is this: *How funny, creative, ambitious am I relative to others?* You simply can't make that assessment in a vacuum. When Loran lived in The Netherlands, he thought himself outgoing and a pretty good dancer. That changed when he moved to Brazil.

Relativity informs how we see the world. Look at the visual illusion below. Focus on the two center circles. We know they are the

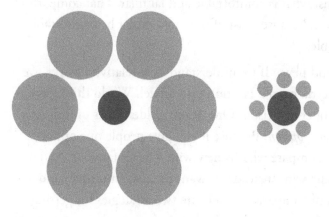

Circles: An optical illusion.

same size. We've measured them before. But that's not what we *see*. The center circle on the right appears bigger because of the context – because the circles surrounding it are smaller.

Relativity doesn't just define how we see ourselves and objects. It also shapes how we see ideas and opportunities. We don't see a new idea in a vacuum. We see it in context. But we neglect this truth when we try to persuade people to embrace change.

Let's imagine you want your employees to adopt a new procedure for reporting expenses. How would you do it? We bet you'd follow a Fuel-based approach by describing the benefits of the new reporting system. You'd explain how the new procedure will save them time, for example.

Do you notice the big problem here? Ask yourself: in this scenario, is relativity (A) working for you, (B) working against you, or (C) a nonfactor? When we pose this question to MBAs, about 75 percent choose option C. Their intuition is that because your employees are only considering one option, relativity doesn't come into play. Alas, not true.

Anytime you present people with a new way of doing things, there is an implicit point of comparison: the status quo. People compare what is new against what is comfortable and familiar. That comparison opposes innovation, because most of us would rather be comfortable than uncomfortable.

Here's the good news. If we understand how relativity works, we can transform Inertia from a Friction into a Fuel. We do this by managing the points of comparison. One of our golden rules of influence is, *never give just one option*. Because if you give people one option, they instinctively compare what is new with what is familiar. And familiar will usually win. Instead, we want to create multiple (and favorable) points of comparison. Here are two strategies for getting relativity to work for you.

Strategy #1: Add an Extreme

Look at the wine list below. What grabs your attention? We bet it is the $125 bottle of wine. It is conspicuous because it is extreme *relative* to the other options on the list. With most bottles costing around $20, the $125 bottle stands out. Why is it there? The restaurant would be thrilled if you splurged on it, of course. But that isn't the real reason it is there. The $125 bottle is there to make it easier for you to justify buying a bottle of wine at the next price level – either the Beaujolais Villages at $44.99 or the Cotes du Rhone at $50.99.

People don't walk around the world with a clear understanding for how much money they are willing to spend on wine. They have some loose sense of wine price, but they mostly look to the context (i.e., the wine list) to guide their choice. If $50 is the most expense wine on the list, ordering a $50 bottle will feel like a bigger splurge.

RED WINE

Pinot Noir, 2008	$17.99
Cabernet Sauvignon	$23.99
Syrah, "La Violette"	$24.99
Bourgogne Rouge, Laforet	$22.99
Beaujolais Villages	$44.99
Morgon, G. Duboeuf	$29.99
Chateau La Chataigniere	$19.99
Chateau Rolland de By	$25.99
Chateau Haut Mondain	$125.99
Chateau Lagarde, St Emily	$25.99
Cotes du Rhone, Les Abei	$50.99

Restaurant wine list: the $125 bottle makes other wines seem reasonable.

But the presence of a $125 bottle makes ordering a $50 bottle seem more reasonable. It's just like the circle illusion. The high-priced wine makes everything else look smaller. The lesson for innovation is that adding a more extreme option makes other options look more reasonable by comparison.

Have you ever noticed the portion options for popcorn at movie theaters? You've got small, medium, large, and extra-large (which should really be called trough-sized). Like the $125 bottle, the extra-large is on the menu for a strategic reason: to move you from a medium to a large.

Idealistic vs. Realistic

A few years ago a commercial waste management company was struggling to grow. They handled garbage delivery for restaurants, malls, and businesses throughout the Midwest. This was a new entrant into a very competitive industry. As the newcomer on the block, it was winning new business by signing short-term, heavily discounted contracts. Initially, their contracts required a minimum one-year agreement. And almost all their clients signed up for (you guessed it) a one-year term. Their goal: increase the number of clients who sign longer-term deals without reducing price.

The waste management company's solution was to offer multiple options. Specifically, it offered one-year, three-year, and five-year contracts. What do you think happened as a result? Companies immediately began signing three-year deals. Compared to a five-year contract, a three-year deal doesn't seem so long. Perception is relative. Changing how people perceived contract length changed their behavior.

There's a detail to this story that offers one of the most important insights around our bad innovation habits. Companies didn't just sign three-year deals. Some actually signed five-year deals, which delighted them, of course. But we were curious. If signing five-year deals is good for the company, why didn't it offer five-year contracts from the beginning? The response was telling: they feared they would be asking too much. Think about that for a moment. When we seek change, we often attempt to sell people not on our ideal option, but rather on what we consider a good but realistic option. We drop the ideal option because we fear we are asking too much. It might be off-putting if we bring it up, we fear. Given what we now know about the psychology of relativity, that's a terrible choice. We should always highlight the ideal path. Because even if the best option is too much, it will make good options look even better.

The two examples above involved price and time, two variables that are easy to quantify. It is easier to use the *add-an-extreme* strategy when the behavior we want to change involves discreet units of measurement – portion size, length of contract, money, etc. But this strategy is almost always available to us, it just takes a little creative thinking.

The fall semester is hiring season at Kellogg. For many years, Loran has been trying to persuade his colleagues in the management department to do something they had never done before – hire a neuroscientist. Loran felt hiring a neuroscientist would help his department in two ways. First, it would keep the department cutting edge. Academic departments can easily get stuck in the past. Behavioral neuroscience is an exciting new field with fertile ideas. Second, it would be a differentiator. Few other management departments have neuroscientists on the faculty. Having one would be a point of distinction.

But these very reasons also cause Friction. It's new. It hasn't been done before. Inertia isn't the only Friction. There are also identity concerns. Would this person fit in with us? Does bringing in a rising star with cutting-edge tools make the current faculty look outdated?

If Loran simply explained the benefits of a neuroscience hire, his colleagues would instinctively compare this new type of hire to traditional hires – the kinds of people the department usually hires and are comfortable with. That is, if Loran follows the conventional approach, relativity will serve as a Friction acting against innovation because it compares a familiar option with an unfamiliar option. What might he do to transform relativity from Friction to Fuel?

Loran realized that to put his idea in a favorable context, he needed to find a way to bucket all the possible neuroscientists into different categories. It occurred to him that you can think in terms of two types of hires: hybrid and pure. A hybrid hire is someone who asks the same kinds of research questions a management scholar typically asks – like how to increase employee motivation or encourage collaboration – but uses a different tool (neuroscience) to answer those questions. And then there's a "pure" neuroscience hire. This is someone who asks more basic questions about human behavior, like how emotion changes the way people process information.

The shortlist of hires he presented to the group were – and were always going to be – hybrid candidates. But the science of relativity suggests that by creating a more extreme category (pure hires) as a reference point, it reduces resistance to the new idea. Now the idea of hiring a hybrid candidate doesn't seem so unknown.

Strategy #2: Highlight Undesirable Options

Let's go back to the expense reporting software example. You don't like the product you are using now and want to find a better option. You know of three products on the market you could choose from. Option A has the same problems as the software your company uses now. According to user reviews, the interface is clunky. It was one of the first products on the market and looks it. So Option A clearly isn't the right choice. Option B is everything Option A isn't. It has a polished look and feel. It gets rave reviews for being user-friendly and has a strong reputation for customer support. But there's a catch: it's double the price you're paying now. It's a better product but the price tag puts it out of reach. And then there's Option C. It also has an excellent user interface. Its customer support isn't as good as Option B but is clearly an upgrade from what you're using now. But unlike Option B, the cost of Option C is a small step up from what you're paying today. Looking at these options, the choice is clear: Option C is the winner.

So how do you sell Option C to your team? The conventional approach is to show the superior option to your colleagues and sing its praises. By now we see the problem with this strategy. We aren't managing the points of comparison. Your employees will reflexively compare Option C to the current product – something that isn't perfect but is at least the devil they know and cheaper than what you're proposing.

To eliminate this Friction, we need to change the points of comparison. Rather than comparing Option C to the existing software, you might compare it to the *inferior* options. Perhaps begin by saying something like, "As you know, there are problems with the reporting software we've been using. There are three other products on the market. I think there's a clear winner. It's called . . . Option C. But to help you make an informed decision, I want to briefly mention the other two products, so you understand their strengths and weaknesses."

By bringing the flawed options to light, you elevate the perceived value of the winning option. Notice that we didn't put all the options on an even footing. We didn't say, "Pick one of these three." Instead, we used the inferior products as *reference points* to put the winning option in context.

The Decoy Effect

Consumer psychology refers to this phenomenon as the *decoy effect*. It goes like this: when there are only two options that force us to make a trade-off between two positive qualities – say cost versus product features – consumers will be guided by their personal preferences. If you are price sensitive, you'll go with the cheaper option. But if offered a third option that has strong product features but is ultimately inferior to the existing option that favors product features, it will lead them to choose the feature-rich option.

To illustrate the concept, here's how the decoy effect could be used to influence people to buy a large rather than a medium popcorn. In one condition, moviegoers were offered a small bucket of popcorn for $3 or a large one for $7. Most chose the small size, suggesting they favored saving money to getting a bigger serving.

But in a second condition, moviegoers were given three options: a small bucket for $3, a large one for $7, and a decoy option: a medium bucket for $6.50. It is a decoy because it costs almost the same as the large but is significantly different size. When presented with these options, the majority of people now chose the large popcorn. But why? Because you get more popcorn for almost the same amount of money. In a relative sense, the decoy makes the large popcorn look like the good deal.

Creating a decoy option is a particularly effective trick of the marketing trade. Some readers will be comfortable with tactics like this, but many will not. We want to draw a clear line between the *highlight inferior options* strategy and creating decoy options. In our software example, you aren't inventing fake options to distort people's thinking. Instead, you are helping them put your favored option in context. Provided people hold the same assumptions you do, the inferior option will reduce the Friction of Inertia. But it is also honest and gives them the ability to make a *more* informed decision.

How Frogs Are Like Wine Lists

Across the animal kingdom, females tend to have discerning taste when choosing sexual partners. The female scarlet tanager (a bird) is looking for a very specific crimson-colored plumage. For the blue-footed booby (another bird), the female is looking for a mate with the best dance moves (if you haven't seen their courtship dance, Google it). For the túngara frog, it is all in the voice. Each spring, hundreds of male túngara frogs gather in pools and begin to sing. These frogs spend most of their lives trying to make as little noise as possible. Bats are a principal predator, and one or two chirps is all a bat needs to echolocate a meal. But despite the risks, these males sing as loudly as they can in hopes of finding a mate.

Amanda Lea and Mark Ryan are two scientists who study the mating calls of frogs (by comparison, our jobs now seem quite boring). When it comes to female túngara frogs, these scholars know exactly what a woman wants. They are looking for a long call (a male that can hold a note), a low-pitch call (they prefer baritones), and a fast call rate (the faster they can repeat the call, the better).

With these three variables – call length, pitch, and rate – Dr. Lea and Ryan can with considerable precision separate the studs from the duds. In 2016, they ran an experiment that speaks to the universal power of relativity. They put a female túngara frog in an aquarium with a speaker in one corner. The scientists played different male mating calls, which varied in impressiveness. They found that if the call came from a first-rate male (which meets her standards), she would hop toward the call. But if the call came from a second-rate male (a mate below her standards), she hopped away from the call.

The scientists wanted to know, what happens when you create an inferior reference point? Are frogs subject to the same laws of relativity? To answer this question, they simply added a second speaker at the opposite end of the aquarium. The scientists simultaneously play two different male calls, one from a second-rate male and one from a third-rate male. Although the second-rate male previously didn't interest the female, when paired with a third-rate male (the inferior option), now the second-rate passed muster.

Relativity in a Nutshell

Here's a super simplified timeline of the change process:

Step 1: Spot a problem.

Step 2: Gather potential solutions.

Step 3: Decide on the best solution (discarding the bad ones and the great-but-unrealistic options).

Step 4: Pitch the solution to your audience.

The principle of relativity shows us that our mistakes happen at Steps 3 and 4. Our habit is to cull the bad options, and at times we may even reluctantly abandon the ideal solution for fear we are asking too much. What we mistakenly present to people is one path – a good (but maybe not ideal) option. You know it is a good option in part because you've considered and discarded inferior ones. You know it. But they don't. Instead, put your ideas in context. Give them a reference point. Because everything is relative.

Overcoming Inertia

The human mind is hardwired to favor the familiar. Yet new ideas ask people to embrace the unknown. This is an ever-present Friction for the innovator. To tame this Friction, we need to transform the unfamiliar into the familiar. Inertia tends to be greatest under two conditions: when the innovation or change represents a major break from the status-quo and when people don't have time to acclimate to change. To determine the level of Inertia that awaits your next idea, ask these three questions.

1. *Does the innovation represent a major break from the status quo or is it a slight tweak on what has been done before?* Radical ideas are likely to run into heavy Inertia headwinds because people inherently distrust and reject unfamiliar and untested ideas.

2. *Have people had time to acclimate to the idea?* If people haven't had time to adjust to new ways of thinking, expect resistance.

3. *Does the proposed change happen gradually or in one big step?* Big, abrupt changes of practice or thinking are the most unfamiliar and therefore produce strong resistance.

If Inertia threatens your innovation, you need to transform the unfamiliar into the familiar. Because as familiarity grows, Friction eases. The aim is to make a new idea feel less like a foreign invader and more like an old friend. This chapter explored two broad approaches for overcoming Inertia, which we call *acclimate the idea* and *make it relative*. When used properly, these techniques can ease resistance to new ideas, and even turn our familiarity bias from a Friction into Fuel for change.

Acclimate the Idea Tactics

1. *Can you increase the amount of time between when people learn about the idea and when they must decide on the idea?* The more time people have to consider the idea, the more familiar it feels.

2. *How often are people reminded of the idea?* Repeated exposure to the idea increases familiarity. Finding opportunities to seed the message will gradually build acceptance for the message.

3. *Can you make the change process gradual rather than disruptive?* When an innovation calls for people to embrace a vastly different

model or way of operating, small steps can help people acclimate to change.

4. *Does the idea fit the prototype, or is it something we have never seen before?* Innovation requires doing things differently. But that doesn't mean every aspect of the idea has to be a radical departure from the status quo.

5. *Who is the face of change?* A spokesperson who shares the same background or experience with the audience is better than an unfamiliar face. If the face of change is someone the audience knows and likes, even better.

6. *Does the look and feel of your innovation match the audience?* Mirroring, or adopting the same language and style of the audience you are attempting to influence, heightens perceived familiarity.

7. *If people aren't familiar with your idea, what familiar ideas can you compare it to?* An analogy makes new terrain feel familiar.

Make It Relative Tactics

1. *Am I giving people more than one option?* If the answer is no, there's a good chance Inertia is working against you. Instead, create multiple options to turn attention away from the status quo.

2. *Can I add an extreme option?* A more extreme or ambitious option makes all other options look more reasonable by comparison.

3. *Can you use an inferior option as a reference point?* Highlighting inferior options makes other ideas look better by contrast.

5 🔲 Effort

Why We Follow the Path of Least Resistance

The common shore crab, which lives among the rocks and tide pools of the Pacific Coast, has a puzzling habit. It is a surprisingly picky eater. Shore crabs feed on mussels. And much like the story of Goldilocks, shore crabs cast aside mussels with small shells and ignore the large ones. But there's a medium-sized mussel that's just right. On the surface, this seems like a dysfunctional strategy. Why would these crabs skip over so many potential meals? The answer can be found in a model of animal behavior called *optimal foraging theory*.

All living things require nutrients to survive. Unlike plants, animals have the capacity to travel to find the resources they need. Whether they spend their entire life foraging in a small pond or traveling thousands of miles in pursuit of prey, the principle is the same. Animals search their environment to find food.

Mobility has huge advantages. If the immediate area is resource scarce, animals can move on to something better. But mobility has its drawbacks. Movement consumes energy. Optimal foraging theory states that all animals are programmed to find the most efficient way to gather resources. Animals are designed to weigh the costs (energy spent) against the benefits (energy gained) when gathering food to maximize energy intake.

It is this cost-benefit analysis that explains why the shore crab is so selective. Mussel shells are, by design, difficult to open. For the crab, opening shells has two costs. It requires a lot of energy to pry them open. And opening shells causes a lot of wear and tear on a crab's claws. If the crab isn't careful, it can damage or break its claw on a mussel shell. Crabs need their claws to feed, so breaking one is a fatal blow.

Smaller mussels mean a smaller meal for the crab. But the shells of small mussels are still difficult to open, so the energy spent is greater than the energy consumed. Large shells contain a substantially bigger meal. But as mussels age, their shells grow thicker, making them particularly hard to open. Crabs are most likely to break their claws on these shells, thus making feeding on large mussels a risky long-term strategy. It too is a net negative.

Medium-sized mussels carry a different payout. They are no more difficult to open than a smaller shell but yield a bigger meal. The calories the crab gets from these mussels exceeds the Effort, and thus the shore crab focuses exclusively on them.[1]

Like the shore crab, humans are highly sensitive to energy expenditure. We are programmed to find and favor the path that brings the most rewards for the least Effort. This design feature is called the *law of least effort*.

When we first encounter a new idea or innovation, our minds instinctively calculate the cost of implementation. The greater the Effort, the stronger the resistance. Unfortunately, innovation generally requires some form of Effort. Learning a new work procedure requires Effort. Unlearning old habits requires Effort. Navigating an unfamiliar website requires Effort. Sifting through new product options requires Effort. Setting up meetings to discuss a new proposal requires Effort. The Effort associated with innovation is a psychological Friction that undermines the appeal of new ideas.

The Law of Least Effort

Though we often aren't aware of its influence, the instinct to minimize Effort is perhaps the most powerful psychological force operating on our decisions. Think about your daily commute to work and all the decisions that go into it. The gas station you use, the route you take, even the mode of transport you select (car vs. public transportation), all of these decisions obey the law of least effort. Your first concern is convenience and efficiency. You likely choose the gas station closest to your home, take the fastest route, and drive your own car because these are the easy and efficient options. They are the choices that minimize personal cost.

The law of least effort states that people over time will follow the path that provides the greatest rewards for the least possible Effort. This principle was first proposed in 1949 by Harvard linguist George Zipf (also known as Zipf's law). As we all know, language changes over time. Zipf's insight was that the evolution of language isn't random. Just as water flows downhill, words and phrases simplify over time. Take the word "goodbye." In England in the 1500s, it was customary to wish someone farewell with the four-syllable phrase, "God be with ye." By the 1600s, the written form of the phrase had been abbreviated to "God b'wi ye." By the 1700s, the phrase was shortened to three syllables and became "God b'ye." A hundred years later, it took on the two-syllable "good-bye." And by the 1900s the hyphen was dropped to form "goodbye." Today, "bye" has now become the standard.

Over the course of history, words and phrases shorten because we naturally find the easier path. "Math" is easier to say than "mathematics" and therefore "math" has largely rendered "mathematics" obsolete. The tendency toward ease and efficiency occurs even at the expense of the original meaning. You've likely heard the expression, *Jack of all trades*. But that expression began as, *jack of all trades, master of none, though oftentimes better than master of one*. The original expression praises the generalist. The expression was later condensed to *jack of all trades, master of none,* which implies that a generalist doesn't know very much at all. And finally, the phrase was condensed further to its current version *jack of all trades,* which again praises the qualities of a generalist.

Simplification isn't the only way language evolves, but it is one of the principal ways words and phrases mutate over time. It is revealing that language doesn't flow in the opposite direction. There are very few examples of words or phrases getting longer with time. Because that runs against our nature.

The evolution of language looks quite similar to the shifts in the American retail landscape over the last 150 years. As towns and cities first developed, Americans bought goods in small stores. Most Americans lived on rural farms, which meant having to travel into town to do their shopping. This was the age of the mom-and-pop shops on main street America. But then Sears made it easier. Their mail-order catalog meant you could shop from the comfort of your home. When Americans moved to the suburbs, department stores and malls became the most efficient way to buy goods. Everything you needed was in one convenient location and you didn't have to wait weeks for your stuff to arrive by mail. Next came Walmart and other big-box stores. And now we are in the age of Amazon and one-click shopping.

Like language, people are constantly seeking more efficient ways to buy goods, and they are surprisingly willing to embrace new modes of shopping when an easier way presents itself. At some point we will find yet another easier path. A new technology like AI assistants or drone delivery will reduce the Friction of shopping online, transforming retail all over again.

Friends of Convenience

The law of least effort rules another important part of our lives – our social relationships. We like to think we select our friends based on meaningful criteria like their virtues, abilities, and shared experiences. In reality, most of our friendships form through ease and opportunity. Scholars call this the proximity principle. The proximity principle is the idea that our friendships are, to a surprising degree, based on convenience. In the workplace, we spend time with colleagues whose office or cubicle is nearby. As distance increases, frequency of interaction plummets. In fact, research on workplace interaction has shown that once distance between two colleagues surpasses 160 feet, there is almost no communication or collaboration whatsoever. Email does little to break this pattern because you typically email people that you already know.

Some of our most meaningful friendships are those we made in college. It turns out that the proximity principle is the driving forces there, too. People might like to think that the friends they made in college were based on a deep, meaningful connection. But you are "picking" friends mostly by proximity. It's a good bet that most of your friends in college happened to be people who lived in your freshman-year dorm. And which of those friends from college do you keep after graduation? Probably the handful that live in the same city you do.

The preference for the easier path is so fundamental, our perceptual system is engineered to make easier options look more appealing.[2] People assume that they perceive the world as it really is. But that isn't so. Consider this elegant study. Participants viewed a screen with a cloud of dots moving either to the left or to the right. Participants were given a joystick and were instructed to move the handle on the joystick to the left if the clouds were moving to the left or move the joystick to the right if the clouds were moving to the right. It's a simple test that all participants passed with flying colors. But in another condition, the researchers added a subtle manipulation. The joystick was rigged so that it was slightly harder to move the handle to one side than the other. The researchers discovered that if moving the handle to the right was more difficult, people started seeing left-moving dots, even when the dots were actually moving to the right. Participants had no idea they were being manipulated. They were completely convinced the dots were moving in the direction of least resistance.

Findings like this are called *motivated perception*. Other studies have found that when people are wearing heavy backpacks, distances look greater and hills look steeper than when people are backpack-free. Such built-in perceptual illusions have an evolutionary advantage. If you are apple picking, you should favor the low-hanging fruit because it takes less Effort to gather. Our cost-sensitive mind is designed to make the low-hanging fruit look the juiciest to nudge us to follow the economical path.[3]

The Primacy of Effort

The law of least effort has enormous implications for innovation. It suggests that when people consider a new idea or opportunity, the first consideration isn't the benefits or value of the idea. The primary concern is the cost of action.

Consider the way our consumption of creative products like movies, TV, and music has changed over time. Let's start with music. Our parents listened to better music than we do – at least in terms of sound quality. Today, most people listen to music by streaming it on their phone through cheap air buds. Listening to music this way is vastly easier than previous music platforms. From our phones we have immediate access to almost every piece of music ever recorded. But this convenience comes at the cost of sound quality. All streaming services use audio compression to make the files smaller. Audio compression literally discards parts of the music the artist wanted you to hear in order to achieve smaller file size.

Everyone wants great-sounding music, but, when push comes to shove, not at the expense of convenience. Movies tell the same story. The best home entertainment systems don't come close to the viewing experience one gets at a movie theater. But now that people can stream videos from home (or on their phone), that's becoming the standard way to watch movies.

Data on hiring decisions also supports the primacy of Effort perspective. When managers are asked to choose between a candidate who is highly competent but difficult to work with or someone who is less competent but easy to work with, people *say* they would pick the former. But in actual hiring decisions, people consistently favor the easy-to-get-along-with candidate over the difficult-but-superior candidate.

To demonstrate Effort's dominance over value, we asked MBA students if they'd be willing to fill out a five-minute survey. For every student who said yes, we would donate $3 to a charity. But we varied the charity. Half were told that completing the survey would raise money for a local dog shelter. The others were told that the money would go to an altogether different charity: the Chicago Herpetological Society. For the uninitiated, herpetology is the study of reptiles and amphibians.

Not surprisingly, people were a lot more willing to volunteer to help dogs than frogs, because the average person cares a lot more about dogs. This outcome speaks to the value of Fuel. People are more likely to say yes to an idea that they value or consider important. If you are able to elevate your idea in the eyes of the audience from a frog (low value) to a dog (high value), your idea is more likely to succeed.

In another class we ran the same experiment with one important difference. We asked for 20 minutes of their time, not 5 minutes. How do you think the more effortful request changed the outcome? The rate of people saying yes declined significantly. That's not surprising. What is surprising is that people no longer had a preference between frogs and dogs. There was no meaningful difference in rate of compliance between the dog and frog conditions. Does that mean people in this group didn't value dogs more than frogs? Of course not. We call this a *crowding-out* effect. People still care more about dogs than frogs, but the cost of the request overwhelmed all other considerations. This might seem like a silly demonstration. And in some sense it is. But it also exhibits people's willingness to put Effort (in this case, time) ahead of other considerations. If your innovation demands a lot of people, you're going to face a lot resistance even if people value the very change you're trying to create.

The primacy of Effort challenges a lot of conventional business calculations. Take customer service. What drives customer loyalty? When 100 customer service heads were asked this question, 89 of them said their main strategy was to exceed expectations. They described Efforts to "wow" customers by going above and beyond. But an in-depth study on customer loyalty defies this view. The study asked 75,000 people to identify the companies they feel the most loyalty for. And then they ask them a series of questions to determine why.

They found that Fuel-based tactics designed to exceed a customer's expectations, such as offering a refund or a small product giveaway, didn't build loyalty. Instead, they found that reducing Frictions commonly experienced during a customer service interaction (like having to explain your problem to several different people) does.

This insight should fundamentally change the way companies look at customer service. The question shouldn't be: how do we delight the customer? The question should instead be: how do we make the interaction easy for the customer?[4] Posing this question can lead to new possibilities and priorities. South Africa's Nedbank recently made reducing customer Effort the foundation of its customer service department. Nedbank created the "Ask Once" promise, a guarantee that the customer will have to interact with only one representative to resolve a problem.

Changing the Effort Calculus

The implication of the law of least effort is clear: reducing the cost of a new idea will make people more open to that idea. That makes Effort big business. Each year, the World Bank measures the ease of starting a new business in countries throughout the world. The Effort varies considerably from country to country. New Zealand was ranked the easiest country in the world to start a business in 2020 (followed by Singapore, Hong Kong, Denmark, South Korea, and the United States). If you hope to start your own business in New Zealand, it takes just a single form and an average of four hours of your time. In India, which ranks 63 on the list, it requires an average of 17 days to start a business (and a heck of a lot more than one form). If you are a hopeful entrepreneur in Chad, which ranks near the bottom of the list, you would need approval from nine different agencies, which takes on average 62 days to complete.

Not surprisingly, the amount of Effort that goes into starting a business is a huge factor in determining people's willingness to start their own company. Countries near the top of the list have nearly four times the entrepreneurial activity as those in the bottom half. If you want to increase innovation in your country, a Fuel-based mindset will lead you to create reforms and opportunities that incentivize starting your own business. What people tend to neglect are the Frictions that stand in the way.

Even seemingly insignificant changes to the Effort calculus can have a big impact on people's behavior. A recent experiment is a case in point. People signed up for the opportunity to have their IQ measured. The researchers explained that the test would have three phases. First, participants would take a 30-minute IQ test. Next, there would be a 10-minute break to let them rest. Finally, participants would complete a second IQ test.

In reality, the experimenters weren't interested in the IQ results. They were actually interested in what the participants did during the break. Once participants completed the first test, an experimenter entered the room with magazines and a bowl of candy. The experimenter explained that during the break the participants should relax and were encouraged to help themselves to the magazines and candy.

But there was a subtle manipulation. The experimenters varied where the bowl of candy was placed. In one condition, the candy was positioned 30 inches from the participant. In the other condition, the candy was placed 10 inches from the participant. At 10 inches, the candy is within immediate reach. At 30 inches, the participant has to lean forward to reach the candy. After the 10 minutes, a researcher removed the candy bowl and weighed it to see how much was consumed. Those 20 inches made a big difference. Participants ate roughly twice as much candy when it was easier to reach. The lesson for innovators is that small changes can have a big impact. Finding ways to make the behavior you want just a little bit easier can change behavior substantially.[5]

Effort Neglect

Although Effort is one of the strongest forces operating on our behavior, people rarely account for it when leading change – a blind spot we refer to as *Effort Neglect*. Loran's research lab has spent years assessing people's intuitions about Effort and its influence.

In one experiment we approached people and asked if they'd be willing to answer a 1-question, 5-question, or 20-question survey. Eighty-four percent said yes to the 1-question survey, a little over half of participants (56 percent) said yes to the 5-question survey, and only 11 percent said yes to the 20-question survey. We then shared the results of the 5-question survey with another group of people. We told this new group that 56 percent of people agreed to answer a 5-question survey. Using this information as a reference point, we then asked this group to estimate how many people would say yes when the request involved a 1-question or 20-question survey. Presumably, more than 56 percent should say yes to a 1-item survey and less than 56 percent should say yes to the 20-item survey.

Participants predicted that 59 percent would say yes to the 1-item survey and 32 percent would say yes to the 20-item survey. In other words, people thought making it easier would make people slightly more willing to say yes (from 56 to 59 percent), and they thought adding 15 additional questions would make people less inclined to say yes (from 56 to 32 percent).

The results make two things clear. People understand that Effort matters. But they have little understanding how much it matters. In this experiment, the amount of Effort in the request was the primary driver of behavior. Effort was far more influential than people anticipated. This blind spot for Effort matters a great deal for innovation. Because if you don't understand the power of Effort, you are going to neglect it when implementing new ideas.

The Uncommon App

The University of Chicago is one of the finest academic institutions in the world. Despite its world-class reputation, the university struggled for years with a surprising problem. Compared to peer schools like Harvard, Princeton, and Yale, the University of Chicago received far fewer college applications. For example, in 2005 Princeton received 28,000 college applications. Chicago received fewer than 4,000.

That's a big problem. College rankings are determined in part by selectivity. The low applicant numbers meant Chicago was admitting a much higher percentage of students, which dragged down the ratings. Whereas peer schools accept around 5 percent of applicants, Chicago was closer to 40 percent. Although college presidents and deans like to downplay the meaningfulness of college-ranking systems created by *US News* and other outlets, there is no denying their impact and importance. The ratings are the main way parents and students learn about the prestige of a university.

The questions for the University of Chicago were, why are applications so low, and how do we fix it? The view of many of the faculty was that the school's reputation for academic rigor scared students away. The school's unofficial motto is, "Where fun goes to die." But academic rigor is also a core value of the school. Changing that would remove the very thing that makes the school special. Other's felt that not being one of the "Ivies" put it lower on students' wish list.

It turns out, the problem had nothing to do with the school itself or its reputation. The problem was the application process. Most schools use a product called the Common Application. It standardizes the application process for schools. Almost all high school students apply to multiple colleges (five schools is the average). Being able to send one application to all of them is a huge time saver.

But the University of Chicago didn't use the Common Application. They were known for having a distinctive application process, which centered on provocative essay questions. Here's an example:

> Who does Sally sell her seashells to? How much wood can a woodchuck really chuck if a woodchuck could chuck wood? Pick a favorite tongue twister (either originally in English or translated from another language) and consider a resolution to its conundrum using the method of your choice. Math, philosophy, linguistics . . . it's all up to you (or your woodchuck).

If you are a college applicant looking to attend one of the elite schools, you can write one essay and submit it to all of the top schools in the country, except one – University of Chicago. To apply to it, you have to write an additional essay and application. From a cost-benefit perspective, the considerably higher admission rate meant that Chicago was the easiest of the elite schools to get accepted into. We suspect most economists would argue that the one or two days it takes to write a new essay is worth the 40 percent chance of carrying that school on the top of your resume for a lifetime.

In 2009, the University of Chicago hired a new president. He made the controversial decision to break with tradition and adopt the Common Application. The next year, applications increased from 5,000 to 33,000.

The key to dramatically increasing enrollments wasn't a Fuel-based solution. It didn't require huge investments in campus beautification initiatives. It didn't mean putting in a state-of-the-art climbing wall. The key was to make the application easier.

This story highlights the power of Effort and the danger of underestimating it. We all understand that more Effort makes a task less appealing. But what is very difficult for the innovator to comprehend is Effort's true force. The University of Chicago faculty knew the uncommon app deterred some people from applying. What nobody understood was the magnitude of the Friction. The uncommon app wasn't part of the problem, it *was* the problem. If they had understood it, they would have abandoned the uncommon app years ago.

When Effort Is Valued

People don't always choose the path of least resistance. There are many contexts in which people actively seek out the road less traveled. Fast food is a lot more convenient than cooking an elaborate meal at home, but we occasionally choose the latter. Here we highlight four common situations where Effort is valued.

When the Experience Is an End in Itself

Sex, like any physical act, requires Effort. But sex is a pleasurable activity. More vigorous sex is generally considered better sex because the experience itself gives pleasure. The same is true of video games. Many are extremely demanding. But people put incredible time, attention, and mental Effort into these experiences because they are so enjoyable.

Virtue Signaling

Effort is a way to demonstrate commitment to a cause or signal one's virtues. How much time you spend volunteering each month is a strong signal of your commitment to humanitarianism. Doing more gives you greater bragging rights.

Effort as Quality

People (often mistakenly) associate more work with better quality. People see a painting that took years to paint as having greater value than one that took a few days. For this reason, researchers love to mention how much work went into collecting data. It's irrelevant. But it gets emphasized because other scholars associate more work with better quality.

Cure for Boredom

People will often seek out physical and mental exertion as a cure for boredom. Boredom is a negative emotional state that people try to avoid. Engaging in a challenging task can offer relief.

6 🔲 Overcoming Effort

How to Build Aerodynamic Ideas

One of the greatest public health challenges facing the world today is access to clean drinking water. Roughly 30 percent of the world's population lacks access to safe water. The result is heartbreaking. The World Health Organization estimates that 750,000 children die each year as a result of drinking unsafe water.

Treating water with chlorine is the most common method for water purification. In the US, 98 percent of public water treatment plants use chlorine to make tap water safe to drink. In developing nations that lack water treatment infrastructure, aid organizations routinely distribute bottles of chlorine to families for water purification. Chlorine bottles are a reliable and cost-effective method for preventing waterborne illness. Unfortunately, very few people actually use them. Only about 10 percent of households that are given chlorine bottles regularly put them to use.

If you dig into the problem, you quickly begin to see why. Gathering and treating water is an exhausting process. First, the water needs to be collected. You travel, often on foot, to a town well or other public watering source. Then you must carry the water back home. Once home, you must treat the water with chlorine. This entails measuring and adding the right amount of chlorine into the water – if you use too little it is ineffective and unpleasant if you use too much. And then you must wait. Chlorine needs time (about 20 minutes) to purify the water.

Innovations for Poverty Action, a nonprofit led by behavioral scientist Michael Kremer, set out to increase chlorine use by designing a system that would streamline the water purification process. Their first test site was in Western rural Kenya. Rather than giving people chlorine bottles for personal use, they instead installed chlorine dispensers at public water sources. The idea was to have people add the chlorine as soon as they filled their water containers. Having people add chlorine to the water before they journeyed home removed one of the major Frictions – waiting for the chlorine to take effect. Now the water was purified as soon as they arrived. The chlorine dispenser had additional Friction-reducing features. Villagers commonly use a five gallon "jerrican" to collect the water. The dispensers were designed to release the exact amount of chlorine needed for one jerrican. Villagers simply had to place their bucket under the dispenser and turn the crank once to release a perfectly measured amount of chlorine. This design feature removed another major inconvenience – having to measure the right amount of chlorine. A final design feature was to paint the dispenser a bright color. Making it visible made it easier to remember to add chlorine.

The results were astounding. When given the individual bottles, they found that only 14 percent of families were consistently purifying their water. But when the same families were given access to a public dispenser, the rate of families drinking clean water jumped to 61 percent – a change that endured over the two years the program was measured. The organization Evidence Action has since expanded the program, installing more than 25,000 dispensers across Kenya, Malawi, and Uganda. Evidence Action estimates that the public dispensers have brought clean water to over 4 million people.

The Innovation for Poverty Action group accomplished these extraordinary results by doing two things well. They diagnosed the Friction points. And once they understood them, they then came up with creative solutions for removing their drag on behavior. When taming Effort-based Friction, we are in essence asking ourselves two basic questions. What makes this behavior difficult to perform? And how can we make it easier? This chapter shares techniques for answering both of these questions.

Effort Defined

Before we can reduce Effort, we need to understand what people mean by it. What attributes of an idea or initiative make it easy or difficult to perform? Effort has two dimensions, one obvious and one not. The obvious and intuitive dimension of Effort is *exertion*. Exertion captures how much energy goes into a task or behavior. Writing a 50-page document requires more exertion than a 5-page document.

A second dimension of Effort is *ambiguity*. If exertion captures the amount of work that goes into achieving a goal, ambiguity reflects whether people know how to achieve the goal. Think about the first explorer to navigate new terrain, or a rat exploring a maze for the first time. If you don't know the way, you have to discover the path yourself. That means trial-and-error. It means false leads and dead ends. Ambiguity is a critical dimension of Effort because a lot of ideas that appear easy to the innovator are shrouded in ambiguity for everyone else.

Imagine any approval process in a company. At an academic institution, it might be the process of getting a new course approved. Effort in the approval process is the combination of exertion and ambiguity. Exertion would capture the amount of work that goes into getting approval. At some institutions, it is relativity easy – just send an email to your department chair describing the course. But that's not the norm. At most institutions we have seen, getting a new class approved is a tedious, bureaucratic undertaking.

Ambiguity reflects whether the approval process is well understood. If a professor is eager to create a new class, does she know how to make it happen? And if she doesn't, does she know who to talk to to get the information she needs? And if she does reach out to colleagues, is she getting consistent or contradictory information? In our experience, the answer to these questions is often "no." If people don't know where to go to get information, it's hard to get started. The confusion surrounding the task is often a bigger hurdle than the actual work.

Understanding the dimensions of Effort is important because they serve as the foundation for overcoming it. Ambiguity is overcome through a process we call *create a roadmap*, while exertion is transformed through a process we call *streamline the behavior*.

Create a Roadmap

One of the now-forgotten challenges of World War II for the US government was its staggering expense. The US spent roughly $300 billion during the war. To put that number in perspective, that's twice as much as the government spent in its *entire* existence before the war. To raise the money needed to fund the war Effort, President Franklin D. Roosevelt and his advisors decided to turn to private citizens for help. America would fund the war through the massive sale of war bonds.

But that would require millions of Americans to buy them. So the US government recruited the best Madison Avenue advertisers to promote the campaign. Posters played a big role in pushing bond sales. As you might expect, the posters leaned heavily on emotional Fuel to trigger buying. One classic poster depicted a wounded soldier on a battlefield asking the question: "Doing all you can, brother?"

Another showed a proud fighter pilot in flight with the caption: "You buy 'em, we'll fly 'em!" Other ads focused on people's fear of the enemy. One poster depicted a Nazi soldier leering at a young girl. The ominous caption read: "Don't let her fall into enemy hands."

It turns out, the slogans that pulled on heart strings weren't the most effective. The fear tactics weren't, either. The most effective slogan wasn't Fuel-based at all. The best slogan didn't explain *why* Americans should donate. The best slogan explained *when* people should donate. The poster depicted employees working in an office with the caption: "Buy them when the Solicitor at your workplace asks you to sign up." The tagline proved to be so effective that the message was soon put on every war bond poster. The result: the sale of war bonds doubled.

Why would a message that didn't inspire patriotism or fear of the enemy outperform those that did? Because it gave people a roadmap. It smoothed the path to donation by telling people when to do it. Think of the Friction not having a map creates. If you don't know that you should buy war bonds from the Solicitor when she visits your office, you might not make time for her when she visits. Or perhaps you put it off, thinking you'll do it after next month's paycheck. The ambiguity of how and when to donate overwhelms the desire to help.

Another early example of the power of roadmapping involved a campaign to bolster tetanus inoculations. A group of psychologists were tasked with designing a message that would convince people to get a tetanus shot, something a lot of Americans fail to do. A variety of messages were created based on different theories of persuasion. One emphasized the benefits of the vaccine, while another stressed the risks and life-threatening consequences of the disease. But like the war bond example, the messages that focused on Fuel weren't the most effective. A third message took a very different approach. It simply showed a map highlighting a local clinic where you could get a tetanus shot, and prompted people to find a time in their schedule that week when it would be feasible to stop by the health clinic. Only around 3 percent of people who received the Fuel-based messages were persuaded to get inoculated. But 28 percent of people who received the roadmap-message ended up getting a tetanus shot.

A similar approach has been successful in get-out-the-vote campaigns. Elections come down to voter turnout. Billions of dollars are spent each year to encourage people to vote. Most of these campaigns focus on *why* people should vote. They stress the importance of voting. Predictably, what campaigns ads aren't designed to do is alleviate the burden of voting. And the Effort associated with voting is a huge factor when it comes to voter turnout. The distance from your home to the poll is a significant predictor of voting likelihood. So is having small children. Not because procreation dents civic duty. It's because all the day-to-day Effort that goes into raising children – making them breakfast, getting them dressed, taking them to school, picking them up from school, etc. – makes getting to the polling station a lot more difficult compared to someone who just has to feed and dress himself.

But when interventions do focus on reducing the ambiguity of voting, they tend to outperform traditional campaigns. Todd Rogers, a behavioral scientist at Harvard's Kennedy School of Public Policy, compared the effects of a conventional voter outreach program with an ambiguity-reducing approach during the 2008 election cycle. Roughly 300,000 people were contacted. One group was encouraged to vote using a standard script used by the Democratic National Committee (DNC). It focused on the high stakes of the upcoming election. Another group was given the same high-stakes script, but also included a section that focused on the logistics of voting. Voters were asked three questions: When in the day will you vote? How will you get to the polling place? Where will you be coming from when you leave for the polling station?

Receiving the conventional script increased turnout by 2 percentage points. Receiving the conventional script plus the roadmap increased turnout 4 percentage points. In other words, adding three short questions *doubled* the effectiveness of the DNC's best voter turnout script. Let's put that two-point increase in context. In the 2012 presidential election, this increase would have flipped outcomes in Florida, Ohio, and North Carolina.

What makes roadmapping so effective? One benefit is that it cuts down on the cost of exploration and clears a path to action. When we ask leaders to identify the behavior they want to see more of from their employees, the same buzzwords surface, time and again. For many leaders, it's innovation. One executive wrote, "I'm constantly encouraging people to innovate, but it doesn't happen. I've even offered incentives. No matter what I say, my people seem fine with the way things are." In sales, it's often devoting time to building leads. Bosses know their people should be out in the community making connections, but instead, bosses complain, their sales staff spends all their time on existing clients and not on building their network. In many large organizations, the buzzword is collaboration. Leaders fret about how siloed their departments have become.

In response to these complaints, we like to give executives a homework assignment: write down when in the day, week, or month the behavior you want to see more of should actually take place. If you want your sales staff out in the field building leads, when and how should that happen? If it's a daily activity, when in the day? And how does it happen? Are there events they should attend? Or conferences? And how is cross-functional collaboration going to take place? Do people know each other well enough to have a discussion? And if so, is there time and space for that discussion to take place?

In most organizations where innovation, lead generation, and collaboration are scarce, executives struggle to answer these questions.

Their objection to this point is that employees should show initiative and answer these questions for themselves. Fair enough. But if there's no obvious path for the behavior to occur, it seldom will. A lot of employee behavior that looks like apathy is really just ambiguity.

Thinking about the when and how of behavior helps people think through the logistical barriers blocking our intentions. To a Fuel-based mindset, logistical issues like scheduling complications will seem like a trivial concern. But to someone who understands the power of Effort, these obstacles are a central concern.

FedEx Days

A beautiful example of roadmapping a behavior comes from Atlassian, an Australian software company that develops a wide variety of project-management tools. Companies like Nike, Coca-Cola, Netflix, and Google rely on their products to manage their most important projects. Atlassian, like every other software development company, holds up innovation as a core value. As it must. Atlassian must continually come up with creative solutions for companies' emerging problems.

But carving out time to think of the products for tomorrow is difficult when daily demands fill your plate. So Atlassian came up with a cultural ritual that creates a window of opportunity for innovation – the behavior needed to be successful — to happen. Each quarter, teams are formed and employees are given 24 hours to produce a new concept or idea. The only rule is that it can't be a product idea they are currently working on. They call these one-day bursts of innovation FedEx days, because teams have to deliver something overnight.

Leadership at Altassian doesn't try to *inspire* innovation through speeches and incentives. Instead, they have created a practice that builds innovation into the system. FedEx days have been so successful for Atlassian that they now teach the practice to other companies who are looking to innovate.

If-Then Triggers

Another benefit of roadmapping is that it helps people remember to perform the act. Simply forgetting to carry out the behavior (as opposed to active resistance) is a big reason people fail to embrace new ideas. For example, 70 percent of women in a study who failed to perform a breast self-examination cited forgetting as the primary explanation. Roadmapping tackles forgetfulness by creating a clear link in memory between a future moment (e.g., when the Solicitor visits your office) and the correct behavioral response in that moment (e.g., buy war bonds). These moment-behavior pairs often have an "if-then" relationship. If situation X occurs, then do Y."

Loran's real estate agent, Tony G, is a case in point. Loran has referred nearly a dozen work colleagues to Tony. One reason is that Tony is very good at what he does. He knows the Chicago market, goes above and beyond for his clients, and is a lot of fun to work with. In other words, he brings a lot of Fuel to the table. But there's another important reason. Tony did something really clever. When Tony asked Loran to refer him to others (as most any real estate agent would do), he said, "If you are looking to do something nice for a new colleague just starting at Kellogg, ask them if they need a real estate agent. You know I'll take good care of them."

That positioning did two small but powerful things. Loran, like most people, wants to support incoming colleagues and build positive relationships with them. Tony made it easy for him to be a good colleague by creating a clear path. Tony also created a clear window of opportunity for him. He didn't just suggest that Loran refer his colleagues to Tony. Instead Tony said, "When you first meet a new colleague, ask if they need an agent." In essence, he created an if-then trigger to make the idea top of mind. Each time Loran has a "get to know you" conversation with a new colleague, he automatically asks if she needs a real estate agent because it effortlessly comes to mind.

At Atlassian, innovation happens in large part because the usual Frictions and barriers have been removed. Even though creating roadmaps helps people act on their intentions, creating them isn't an intuitive or common practice. Ironically, the tendency to neglect the implementation of new ideas is strongest for people who are deeply committed to an idea. Recent research suggests that people who feel the greatest conviction to act are most prone to neglect the Frictions that might sabotage their intentions. This is because they mistakenly believe their strong conviction is enough to get them across the finish line, no matter the obstacle.[1]

Streamline the Behavior

The other dimension of Effort is exertion. Exertion captures the size and severity of the roadblocks standing in your way. The greater the Effort required, the stronger the resistance to change. If the Effort in your idea is causing resistance, your job is to find ways to make change easier. Your goal is to remove drag by making your idea sleek and aerodynamic. We call this *streamlining*. Streamlining involves knocking down barriers and finding shortcuts.

Streamlining begins by spotting the points of Friction. Sometimes they are self-evident. Having to wait in a long line is a clear and obvious Friction. Other times the Friction is hidden and can only be revealed through careful discovery. Beach House (see Chapter 1) is a good example. The Friction – not knowing what to do with one's old couch – was hidden until the company conducted in-depth interviews with customers.

But you don't have to hire a behavioral designer to find these Frictions. Often a few good questions and a little reflection is all it takes. A case in point. A friend of ours is a professional public speaker. Like any good business owner, he carefully tracks data on his performance. One piece of data he carefully monitors is the number of referrals he generates from a speaking engagement. Referrals are the main way he grows his business, so it is one of his primary metrics for success. Over drinks one evening, he told us about a funny pattern. It was all or nothing. Either a talk generated a handful of leads or none at all. Here's some data he shared.

10/15/19: 0 leads

10/19/19: 6 leads

11/05/19: 9 leads

11/16/19: 0 leads

11/17/19: 4 leads

12/10/19: 0 leads

12/13/19: 8 leads

Why, he wondered, do some engagements produce a bounty of leads and others nothing? Though they don't sound rehearsed, his talks follow a carefully crafted script. So it's not like the performance varies much from talk to talk. After some probing, one of us asked the right question: How do the referrals happen? Do they contact you over email, or do you first meet face-to-face? Almost 100 percent face-to-face, he said. And when does that happen? Immediately after the talk, he answered. He went on to explain that he makes himself available as much as possible immediately after the talk so people can engage with him. Because that's when all the leads seemed to happen. And that's when it hit him. Coffee breaks! The presentations that are leading to referrals are those that have a coffee break or happy hour immediately after the talk. There is, in other words, a clear window of opportunity for connection. In the zero-referral talks, his presentation is followed by *another talk*. His email is prominently displayed in all the leave-behinds, and he ends all his talks by encouraging attendees to follow up with him. But following up with someone when you are feeling inspired and they are in the room with you is easy. Finding a moment to send a thoughtful email asking to set up a time to speak evidently is a bridge too far. This small insight has paid huge rewards. The rule he now follows is, whenever possible, make sure a coffee break or happy hour follows his presentation.

Our approach to streamlining an innovation follows two steps. The first step is to chart the user's journey through the process or experience. We call this creating an *experience timeline*. An experience timeline identifies all the steps a person must take to complete a desired action. Experience timelines are moment-by-moment visual representations, where the pole furthest to the left of the diagram represents the beginning of an experience, and the pole furthest to the right represents its conclusion.

The objective of an experience timeline is to help innovators visualize the moments of Friction that inhibit change. "Positive experiences" on the timeline reflect moments that generate a high degree of user satisfaction or positive sentiment. These moments signal experiences in a user's journey that innovators may wish to further amplify. "Negative experiences" are moments in which users must endure an unusual amount of Effort or dissatisfaction. These negative moments on the timeline present clear opportunities for streamlining.

To construct experience timelines, we begin by asking users to reflect on their recent journey through a particular experience – naming the specific moments along the way that they feel mattered the most. We then ask them to *draw* their personal experience along the timeline in the form of a "sine wave," marking how they felt

EXPERIENCE
TIMELINE

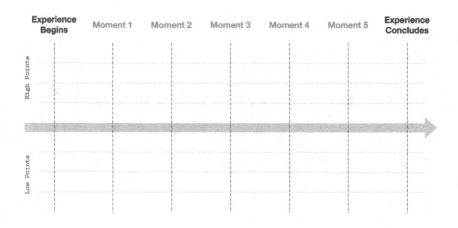

Experience timeline.

(positive, negative, or neutral) at those particular moments in the journey. The height and depth of the wave indicates the intensity of the high points and low points in the journey. After completing 7–10 experience timelines with different users, clear patterns will begin to emerge, helping us focus our attention on streamlining the moment(s) most in need of improvement.

Let's return to the example of using chlorine pills to purify water. If you are a nonprofit dedicated to increasing access to clean drinking water, giving people chlorine tablets seems like an *easy* fix. On the surface, it requires one simple step: add chlorine tablets to your water. The Innovation for Poverty Action (IPA) group realized that the behavior was more difficult than it appeared. IPA outlined five distinct moments of Effort in the water purification process. Moment

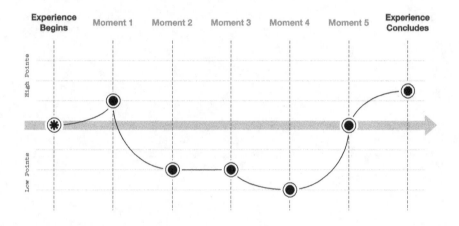

EXPERIENCE TIMELINE

Example

Comparison of several experience timelines shows areas needing improvement.

1 is to make the journey to water source. Moment 2 is the act of gathering the water. Moment 3 is the return journey home with the water they have collected. Moment 4 is to measure and add the chlorine dose to the water. Moment 5 is to wait the 20 minutes for the water to purify.

Once the negative moments are identified through the timeline, the next step in streamlining process is to remove them. If the first step of the process is like being a detective who tries to spot the Effort clues, the next step is more like being an engineer who tries to reconstruct the environment to create a smoother path to action. The IPA group saw that the two most costly Frictions in the user's overall experience were the return journey with the water and waiting

EXPERIENCE TIMELINE

Innovation for Poverty

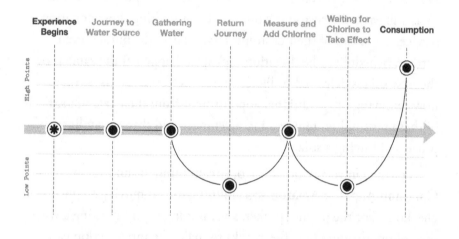

Experience timeline for Innovation for Poverty Action water purification study.

20 minutes for the chlorine to do its job. While they could not eliminate the return journey with the water, they *could* redesign the process so that the chlorine was added to the water at the time it was collected. That way the purification process happens during the journey home, which shaves 20 minutes off the entire process. The key to streamlining (and the benefit of an experience timeline), is to diagnose which *specific* steps in a journey are causing the greatest Friction, thereby focusing your energy and resources on addressing the moments that matter most.

Many of the stories we've shared thus far involve streamlining interventions. Let's go back to Beach House. Their solution made purchasing easier by removing and donating their customers' old sofas. That offer relieves a major Friction. But it's not the only approach Beach House could have taken. Maybe the logistical challenges and expense of picking up and donating old furniture was too costly. In this case, partnering with organizations like Habitat for Humanity or the Salvation Army to remove and repurpose the old sofas still eases the customer's burden. Coordinating these donation services on behalf of their customers would ease the burden even further. Scheduling the donation pickup to happen at the same time the new sofa is delivered really changes the effort calculus – you are now removing one additional appointment from their calendars. Each of these possibilities removes inconvenience and thus streamlines the process of buying a sofa.

For the University of Chicago, streamlining meant moving to the Common App. For Amazon, streamlining meant moving to one-click checkout. For the public speaker, streamlining meant creating a window of opportunity (a coffee break) to make the introduction easier for the audience.

Desire Paths

The shortest distance between two points is a straight line. But the world doesn't always present us straight-line options every time we are trying to get from one place to another. So we invent them. *Desire paths* are human-made shortcuts. You've seen them in public parks and forest preserves. Desire paths are the worn-down grass or dirt trails that we create with our feet when we don't follow the sidewalk or established trail but instead find a shorter, easier path to our destination – because the easier path is the *desired* path.

Desire paths have traditionally been seen as an eye sore. But urban planners are increasingly seeing them as a valuable source of user feedback, adapting sidewalks and trails by paving the desire paths and thereby improving the design. Taking things a step further, some designers are now waiting to create permanent paths until they first see the footpaths people naturally create on their own.

Desire paths also show up in how we engage with products, services, and experiences. When something feels too complicated, slow, or effortful, we create shortcuts and workarounds for ourselves. Like urban planners, many innovators feel frustration when people don't use their ideas in the way they intended. But there is value in spotting the shortcuts people create on their own, because they are signaling to you their desire to find an easier way.

@FAKEGRIMLOCK is a Twitter personality and tech influencer. His persona is that of a robotic tyrannosaurus from the future that tweets in ALL CAPITAL LETTERS, and only in sentence fragments. Despite the ridiculousness of the picture you are now holding in your head, FAKEGRIMLOCK actually dispenses some sage wisdom from time to time. One of our favorite musings from this learned time-traveling dinosaur is about the opportunity in desired paths and shortcuts: "WHERE YOU SEE DUCT TAPE, REPLACE WITH AWESOMENESS."

Streamlining 2.0

Streamlining is an art. Sometimes the solution is obvious. If a 50-page report is too demanding, reducing the requirement to 25-pages will relieve some Friction. But many of the most effective streamlining techniques are often overlooked. Below, we describe two streamlining techniques that all innovators should keep in their toolbox.

Make "No" Harder

Streamlining is generally the process of making the behavior you want easier. Another strategy is to make "no" more difficult. Take scientific publishing. Science rests on the peer review system. When a scientific paper is submitted for publication, other scientists who are knowledgeable about the area are asked to review the paper to determine its merit. But this system only works if other scientists are willing to review. A review takes about a half-day of one's time. And many scholars receive several review requests a month. Not surprisingly, it's difficult to get reviewers. In the conventional format, a scientist receives an email that simply asks whether you accept or decline the invitation. Notice that clicking "no" is just as easy as clicking "yes." A few wise scientific journals have discovered a better way to ask this question. Rather than asking yes or no, they offer these two options: accept the invitation or write the name and email address of a reviewer who can take your place.

Notice that compared to five hours of tedious work, writing down the name and email of another colleague is trivial. Yet it has a huge impact on behavior. Because in that moment when people are deciding whether to say yes or no, it changes the Effort calculus. It adds Friction in the form of exertion and ambiguity. You have to think about who would be a suitable reviewer (sometimes that's obvious, sometimes it is not). Then once you find a reviewer, you have to locate her email address. "Yes" is the easier choice in that moment.

Here's another simple way to put this idea into action. When trying to get people's buy-in, rather than ask: "What do you think of this idea?" Ask instead: "Do you like this idea, or do you have something better in mind?" That slight reframe changes the demands of "no." Rather than just rejecting an idea, it requires you to come up with better alternatives. That simple Friction will move a lot of people to "yes."

Make It the Default

The goal of streamlining is to remove obstacles to make the behavior you want easier to implement. What if you could take this a step further? What if you could change the Effort calculus so that the behavior you want from people isn't just easier, but actually required no Effort at all? That's precisely what happens when you make the behavior you want the default option. A default simply means the outcome that occurs if no action is taken.

If there were awards for the most powerful tools in the behavioral sciences, defaults would take first prize. Consider some evidence. For years, Disney World tried to encourage kids to pick healthier options at its theme park. But all the marketing and messaging that promoted fruits and vegetables did, as you can imagine, very little to steer kids away from pizza and soda. But then they tried a different approach. Disney changed the default choices in the kids' meal. Rather than having a sandwich automatically come with fries and a soda (as it had in the past), the default option became fruit and juice. Kids could request fries and soda (at no additional cost) but would have to actively request it. Most kids followed the path of least resistance. Changing the default reduced calorie intake by 21 percent, reduced fat by 40 percent, and lowered sodium by 45 percent.

Changing the default has the power to save lives. In Germany, only 12 percent of the population is on the organ donation registry. That's quite low when you consider that Austria, Germany's next-door neighbor, has a 99 percent sign-up rate. Denmark is even worse than Germany, with less than 5 percent on the organ donation registry. Yet Sweden sits at 85 percent. What accounts for this difference? In countries where organ donation is low, you are born into the world a nondonor and have to fill out a form to get on the registry. In those where it is near universal, it's the exact opposite: you are born a donor and you have to opt out to get off the registry. Getting on or off the registry is not a lot of work. It's simply a matter of filling out a form.

But even when alternative paths are relatively easy, most people follow the path of least Effort.

Recently, an executive in class shared how he used the default principle to handle resistance to change. When leading a new initiative, he would often be overwhelmed by complaints about change. The smallest change to company policy would bring out a chorus of criticism. So he made "yes" the default. His habit was to hold breakfast "office hours." When announcing a new change, he would invite people to sign up for a breakfast if they had questions, concerns, or ideas about the new initiative. He found that people who had legitimate concerns showed up. These are exactly the people he wanted to hear from. But most people who had felt mild resistance because the initiative wasn't familiar or required a little bit of Effort, wouldn't make time to meet. And after they had time to adjust, they got on board.

Harnessing defaults can transform the demands on your time. Think about all the requests you receive from people asking for your help or seeking your advice. This puts you in a difficult position. Most people want to help, but if you say yes to every request, you will exhaust yourself (as many leaders do). Here's where managing the default can be your savior. If you want to help, say yes to the request. But make the person take the first step. For example, if someone wants to pick your brain over coffee, ask them to send you a calendar invite. If someone would like career advice, you might say: "I'd be happy to help. Please send me an email with your resume and a brief description of your career goals."

No matter the request, have them take the first step. Loran lives by this rule to manage student interaction. In his experience, when you ask people to do the smallest thing, 9 out of 10 people never follow up. There are a few people who truly respect your time. And there are others who want your time, but only if it is convenient for them. You only have time for the former. Setting the right default helps you see who truly values your time.

Think Like a UX Designer

Have you ever wondered why certain websites and mobile applications are easier and more enjoyable to use than others? Welcome to the world of user experience (UX) design. UX designers create the interfaces and relationships we have with software products. It's their job to make a digital product feel "intuitive" to its users by removing Effort from the user experience. Thinking like a UX designer can help you spot Frictions and streamline a path to action. Consider these four core UX principles for Effort-reduction inspiration.

Reduce the Load

The more steps required during a user experience, the higher the chances the user will give up on it along the way. Simon King, author and accomplished designer for renowned UX companies like DuoLingo and Abridge AI, points out that each (seemingly innocuous) step in a journey could be *the* step that incites a user to abandon the journey – or, in UX speak, causes them to "bounce."

Consider the simple act of creating a user profile for a new website or mobile application. The more steps a user is required to complete in the process, the higher the likelihood the user will bounce before completion. The bounce could occur in the first few steps of the process (entering a name and email address). It could happen at the third step (adding a phone number) or the fourth (inputting credit card data). Each of these steps is a risk. They create micro-Frictions in which a user might get distracted or pause to reconsider the purchase.

So, what's the solution? Auto-complete. Perhaps one of the most ingenious UX innovations in the last several years. Auto-complete is the bit of code in a digital application that

(continued)

prepopulates data such as your email address, phone number, and even your credit card details into fields requesting that information. Prepopulating this data reduces the number of steps the user must take, which greatly improves the chances that they will complete the sign-up journey.

Design for Simplicity

Just because you *can* add a feature to a product does not mean you *should*. Products that contain a lot of features tend to result in complicated interfaces that overwhelm users, resulting in Frictions of both Effort (time and energy) and Emotion (feeling overwhelmed). The perfect example of the simplicity principle in action is the difference between Google's search page and Yahoo's. Sure, Google's isn't particularly pretty to look at, but there is no ambiguity whatsoever for first-time visitors about how to use it. Its simplicity is one of its lasting competitive advantages in the ever-changing world of search engines. Simon King is careful to highlight that "simple does not *always* mean less. What it really means is designing new experiences in such a way that a user inadvertently making an irreparable error is almost impossible."

Follow Hick's Law

Have you ever been to a restaurant where the menu resembles a phone book because of the overwhelming number of options? Restaurants that have limited menus indulge us in *the luxury of limited choice* – fewer options mean less Effort, and less fear about choosing the "wrong" entree. The same is true in product design. Hick's law (named for psychologist William Edmund Hick) states that the more choices you present to someone, the longer a process will take and the more Effortful it will be for them to make a decision. In UX design, "less is more" because giving a user too many options can be overwhelming.

Provide Progress Feedback

A final principle of UX design is to let people know when they make progress on a website. It can be daunting for an individual to go through an entire user journey, especially when the end of the journey is unclear. Signaling their progress along the way can make the overall experience feel less onerous and less ambiguous. In software design, this type of feedback is provided by confirmation notices and progress bars that help users visualize their advancement through the digital experience. These small moments of reinforcement and affirmation serve as mini rewards for what might otherwise feel like a laborious user journey.

Overcoming Effort

The human mind favors the path of least resistance. When we first encounter a new idea or innovation, our minds instinctively calculate the cost of implementation. The greater the Effort, the stronger the resistance. Unfortunately, innovation generally requires some form of Effort. Effort has two dimensions: exertion and ambiguity. If exertion captures the amount of work that goes into achieving a goal, ambiguity reflects whether people know how to achieve the goal. To determine the level of Effort that awaits your next idea, ask these two questions:

1. *How much physical and mental exertion is required to implement the change?* The more exertion, the more resistance the idea will encounter.

2. *Do people know how to implement the desired behavior, or is the path ambiguous?* A lot of ideas that appear easy to the innovator are shrouded in ambiguity for everyone else.

This chapter explored two broader approaches for overcoming Effort. Ambiguity is overcome through a process we call *create a roadmap* while exertion is transformed through a process we call *streamline the behavior*. The questions below can help you diagnose and eliminate the Effort lurking in your new ideas.

Create a Roadmap

1. *Can you show people how to implement the desired behavior?* If implementing change is shrouded in ambiguity, giving people step-by-step instructions makes the innovation easier to embrace.

2. *Do people know when to perform the desired action?* A clear window of opportunity sets aside time for the innovation and helps people to remember to implement it.

3. *Can you create an if-then trigger?* Simply forgetting to carry out the behavior (as opposed to active resistance) is a big reason people fail to embrace new ideas. An "if-then trigger" tackles forgetfulness by creating a clear link in memory between a future moment and the correct behavioral response in that moment. If situation *X* occurs, then do *Y*.

Streamline the Behavior

1. *What are all the steps (including the seemingly insignificant ones) a person must take to implement your idea?* An experience timeline can reveal the hidden pain points working against innovation.

2. *How can you make the innovation easier to implement?* Remember that removing seemingly small Frictions can produce huge results.

3. *Can you make it more Effortful to say "no" to innovation?* Streamlining is generally the process of making the behavior you want easier. Another strategy is to make "no" more difficult.

4. *Can you change the Effort calculus so that the behavior you want people to perform requires no Effort at all?* If you can make your innovation the default option, it all but guarantees its success.

7 ❤ Emotion

Why the Best Ideas Produce the Most Anxiety

If you have ever baked a cake, chances are, you used a cake mix. Today, 60 million more Americans use a prepackaged mix to make their cakes than those that bake from scratch. The appeal of cake mix isn't hard to understand. Baking a cake from scratch is a lot more work (i.e., Effort), and it requires absolute precision. If the temperature of the oven or the consistency of the batter isn't just right, the cake won't rise. A cake mix removes the hassle and nearly guarantees a perfect result. Without a doubt, it's a wonderful innovation for bakers everywhere.

You would think these benefits would make cake mix the go-to option for all but the most ardent baking purists. Yet when cake mix first hit the market in 1929, it was far from an overnight success. Despite all the clear benefits, it would take 25 years before cake mix would finally catch on.

The problem wasn't the taste. In taste tests, people loved the cakes from a mix every bit as much as they do today. The problem wasn't the price. It's cheaper to use a cake mix than it is to make a cake from scratch. In fact, the problem had nothing to do with cake at all. It had to do with what the cake *represents*. Think for a moment about *why* we choose to make a cake. We don't bake a cake just for ourselves. We bake a cake to celebrate someone else. We bake a cake to express love and affection. We bake a cake to celebrate milestones and achievements. Cakes are the ultimate greeting card for someone we care about. The time it takes to bake a cake demonstrates our care. The cake itself is just an artifact of the sentiment it embodies.

When cake mix was first introduced, using it was seen as a soulless act. Making a cake from a mix was akin to inviting friends over for a home-cooked meal and microwaving them a frozen entrée. To homemakers in the postwar era, baking a cake from a mix symbolically said, "I don't care enough about you to make this myself." That stigma was a major friction to broad adoption. If you baked from a mix, you hoped no one would notice out of fear people would judge you for cutting corners.

By the 1950s, General Mills, the main seller of cake mix at the time, had learned to accept that cake mix would always have a limited appeal. It would never be more than a "plan B" option bakers would turn to when they ran out of time to do it right.

And then Ernest Dichter entered the picture.

Ernest Dichter was a Viennese psychologist who immigrated to the United States to escape the impending war in Europe.[1] Dichter believed that the same principles of psychology that helped identify and treat neuroses could be used to more deeply understand the needs of consumers. The signature invention born out of Dichter's methods was the "focus group."[2] Focus groups create an environment in which research subjects can more deeply express their desires as part of a qualitative discussion with others. This research innovation was a sharp contrast to the prevailing quantitative techniques of the time, such as surveys and polls. Ditcher thought surveys might help illuminate *what* people choose to do, but focus groups help discover *why* they do it – the underlying *motivation* behind those choices.[3]

As legend has it, General Mills hired Dichter to find a way to remove the stigma of cake mix from its Betty Crocker brand. Dichter met with bakers to understand why they were reluctant to use a cake mix.[4] The fear of being judged for not taking the time to bake from scratch was a major issue. But Dichter uncovered a deeper problem that cake mix companies had failed to realize.

Betty Crocker cake mix included all the ingredients you need to make a cake. The only thing a baker had to do before the cake went in the oven was add water. The deeper problem was that using a cake mix didn't *feel* like baking. Not only did the baker not have to do much in the way of work, they didn't even add a single ingredient! Feeling the pride of making something is one of the big reasons why people enjoy baking. Using cake mix stripped them of that pride.

Dichter helped General Mills recognize that the problem with cake mix was the very thing that made cake mix an innovation – using cake mix was too easy. His recommendation was to introduce a small amount of Effort back into the process. For several reasons, some of which are deeply Freudian, Dichter settled on fresh eggs as being the sole ingredient that home bakers should add to the process. Whisking eggs into the premixed batter provided just the right amount of work. It was still much easier than baking for scratch, but allowed home bakers to feel that the cake was "theirs."

Once General Mills removed powdered eggs from the formula and the recipe called for adding eggs, the feeling of accomplishment and satisfaction returned. Users felt that they were actually *baking*. Sales skyrocketed, and American home bakers have never looked back. That's why, to this day, most cake mixes still require bakers to *add eggs*.

Emotional Friction

The history of cake mix demonstrates how emotion can get in the way of innovation. We define Emotional Friction as the unintended negative feelings that inhibit a new idea or innovation. Emotional Friction takes many forms. The anxiety and doubt associated with committing to a new product is a common Emotional Friction. The embarrassment of being a teacher's pet is an Emotional Friction that prevents many school children from displaying their academic potential. Social anxiety is a Friction that keeps introverts from attending valuable networking opportunities. We encounter Emotional Frictions every day, in decisions big and small. Think back to the Chapter 2 story about Army recruitment. That was a story about Emotional Friction. Despite wanting to enlist, many would-be recruits don't because they fear how their mother will react.

Emotional Friction is the exact opposite of what we intend to do. When introducing a new idea, we hope to trigger positive emotions. We want our ideas to fill people with delight, excitement, confidence, etc. But without our realizing it, our audience often has the exact opposite emotional reaction. Even the most promising idea can unintentionally trigger negative emotions that become significant barriers to adoption. When that happens, those negative emotions are Frictions. And, just as with other frictions, the drag of Emotional Friction must be addressed before any real change can occur.

There can be incredible opportunity in spotting the Emotional Frictions that your competitors have missed or failed to resolve. Consider the success of the dating app, Tinder. Before Tinder, online dating was dominated by companies like Match.com and eHarmony. These companies require you to build a detailed profile of yourself, including intimate details like political views, salary, and body type. Once you create a profile, the next step is to search the huge database for potential matches. The final step is to send an email to the people you are interested in.

One clear Friction in the Match.com model is that the process is Effort intensive. People put a lot of work into building the perfect (though not necessarily accurate) online profile. They devote even more time searching for potential matches. And who you search for isn't straightforward. Should you look for someone who lives within five miles from you or do you look further afield? This is one of dozens of choices you must make in customizing your search. Changing any one of those parameters will give you entirely different results. And once you find someone you like, you then have to craft the perfect email. This person might be *the one*. So, people often spend hours writing and rewriting a message they hope will hit all the right notes.

This entire process takes a lot of time and exertion. For some, it's fun and exciting. But for many, it's exhausting. Part of Tinder's success is that it has removed a lot of the Effort from the dating process. You set up a profile in just minutes. Tinder finds candidates for you. And there's no messaging. Just the swipe of a finger.

But making it easier is only part of what makes Tinder so successful. Tinder also figured out how to remove a painful Emotional Friction. If you are using Match.com, you have to reach out to someone when you have no idea if they have any interest in you. Expressing interest in someone takes courage because you are making yourself vulnerable to rejection. Imagine finding a potential date who seems a perfect match. So you send him a thoughtful message asking if he would like to meet for coffee. For a Match.com user, you often get replies likes this:

"I'm looking for someone a little younger."
"Sorry, I don't date Republicans!"
"You're not my type."

Or perhaps worse, you don't hear anything at all. The point is that traditional online dating platforms produce a lot of rejection. Many people drop off sites like Match.com because they find the frequent rejection difficult to bear. Tinder greased the Emotional Friction of online dating by creating a system based on mutual interest.

To have the ability to reach out to someone on Tinder, both people
have to "swipe right" on each other. Mutual interest is established
before people make themselves vulnerable. Tinder's core insight was
that you feel more comfortable approaching somebody if you know
they want you to approach them. Spotting and fixing the pain of
traditional online dating sites helped Tinder (and its many imitators)
to become the dominant model for online dating.

What Is Emotion?

Emotion has a profound influence over our behavior. We
experience emotion as a feeling. But emotion is much more
than a subjective experience. Emotion transforms our thoughts
and actions. Emotion shifts our attention, changes the way we
process information, and alters which ideas and memories we
bring to mind.

Emotions are designed to create adaptive responses to
critical situations we faced in our evolutionary past. Fear, for
example, is triggered when we detect a potential threat in our
environment. The experience of fear initiates the goal to avoid
risk. Fear broadens our visual perception to help us detect
threats (fear literally expands our peripheral vision). And it
readies the body for fight-or-flight action.

Emotion has both a constructive and destructive influence on our lives. Emotion is the root of most self-control
problems. Rage, pride, and fear can lead us to make regretful
decisions. But emotion is also critical for proper human func-
tioning. People who don't feel emotion (usually due to a significant brain injury) struggle to understand and interact with
others and have tremendous difficulty making good decisions.

Hiring Emotion

To better understand Emotional Friction, we first need to start with its mirror opposite – Emotional Value. One of the best frameworks we have found to understand emotional value is the "jobs-to-be-done" theory. Jobs-to-be-done theory was created and coined by product innovator Bob Moesta and was later evolved and popularized in the book *Competing Against Luck* by the late Clayton Christensen, a Harvard Business School professor and innovation thought-leader.

The foundational principle is that people "hire" products and services to deliver three basic needs: functional value (e.g., it will save you time), social value (e.g., it will impress your friends), and emotional value (e.g., it will bring you joy). According to Bob Moesta, "These three dimensions of value are present in each and every decision we make about whether or not to buy or try something new."

For example, when you purchase a new winter jacket, these three values are likely at play in your decision-making in the following way:

Functional value. How warm and dry you feel when wearing the jacket.

Social value. What the style and brand of the jacket may signal about you to others (fashion conscious, wealthy, earthy, hipster, etc.).

Emotional value. How you feel about yourself when you wear it (and even when you see it hanging in your closet).

This framework is not limited to products and services. It applies to any idea or innovation. Consider the impact of Covid-19 on education. In the spring of 2020, schools at all levels rushed to shift their teaching online as the nation went into lockdown. Almost overnight, teachers had to shift their content and instruction to an online environment. Fortunately, videoconferencing technologies such as Zoom and Microsoft Teams were able to scale up to meet the wave of new demand. The functional value of this new technology, though, was only one piece of the puzzle. A second piece—far more complicated and challenging—was getting students and faculty comfortable with the idea of interacting online. In this case, the dimensions of value for teachers are determined by questions like this:

Functional value. Do students learn as well online compared to the traditional in-person format? Does the technology have the right features to meet the different learning needs of the students in class? Is it easy to use?

Social value. How well does it support the interpersonal interactions that students and teachers desire? How does its use make teachers appear to both students and their peers? Could fully embracing this technology make a teacher appear tech savvy? Could reluctance make them look out of touch with the times?

Emotional value. How confident or vulnerable do teachers feel while using this new technology? Does this shift inspire optimism or pessimism about the technology-driven world? Are teachers being set up for personal success or failure?

Jobs-to-be-done theory's major advance was to recognize that value is multifaceted. But if emotion can be the reason why a person chooses to embrace a new idea, it can also be the reason we reject change.

Noah's Animal House

Staci Alonso knows about the healing power of animals. When she lost her fiancé while pregnant with their son, it was her pets that helped her endure a tremendously challenging time in her life. The experience taught her firsthand how the love and affection of an animal can make even the most unbearable life experiences a little more manageable.

Staci has always felt the need to help others through challenging moments. So, in 2003 she joined the board of *The Shade Tree*, a Las Vegas, Nevada – based shelter that provides abused and homeless women and their children with food, shelter, and safety, empowering them to leave dangerous living situations behind. The Shade Tree has been doing this important work since 1989, serving women from all walks of life and communities in the state of Nevada. All were welcome at The Shade Tree – with one significant exception. There were no pets allowed.

To a non-pet owner, this rule might not seem like such a big deal. Perhaps women could give their pet up for adoption or leave it with a friend. But as any pet owner knows, these animals are far more than just pets; they are true friends and providers of unconditional love – something that carries infinitely greater meaning for a woman trapped in an abusive relationship. As Staci told us, "Pets are a huge factor in healing, love, and support. For many abused women, leaving a loved pet behind was simply out of the question." She added, "Emotion drives it," so much so that women would often stay in a dangerous environment simply because they did not want to abandon their pets. These animals were often the only source of warmth, joy, and friendship in their lives. Staci recounts,

> We would watch women pull into the parking lot of the shelter and leave their dog tied to a utility pole, or their cat carrier on the pavement, and then walk to the door. We could see the very moment they read the "No Pets" sign, and then stand around there for a little while, thinking about what to do. They would look at the shelter, then back at their pet, and after several minutes of consternation they would just turn around and head back to where they came from.

The same pattern presented itself on the phone. Staci observed that, "(a woman) would call up and ask us a few questions about the shelter. It would start with basic stuff about the arrival process and checking in. And then, a few minutes into the conversation she would ask, 'Can I bring my dog?' When the shelter said 'no' she would just hang up the phone." After seeing this same story play out dozens of times, Staci decided that removing the emotional barrier of "no pets allowed" was a must.

In 2007, Staci created *Noah's Animal House*, a separate facility built on the grounds of The Shade Tree shelter that offers boarding and pet services for the animals of women seeking the safety of the shelter. Just as The Shade Tree was a safe-haven for women, Noah's Animal House would be a safe-haven for their pets. And because it was on the same property, women could visit and play with their pets while they worked on rebuilding their own lives. No longer would women have to be separated from their greatest sources of love and joy while they healed. They could do it together.

As the story of Staci Alonso and Noah's Animal House demonstrates, Emotional Friction is often revealed when we observe the full "journey" of those we hope to serve – the series of events, motivations, and feelings that led to a moment of change, and the events and feelings that will unfold after that decision is made (or not made). Looking at the journey of a single woman approaching The Shade Tree with a pet would not have highlighted the profound Emotional Friction standing in the way of her progress. But by studying *several* user journeys and looking at patterns across them, the problem (and its source) become readily apparent.

Much like injecting a contrast dye to aid in the clear analysis of a medical image, examining and comparing multiple user journeys help us shine a light on key moments of Friction. This is especially helpful in the identification of Emotional Friction, as it rarely presents itself in traditional forms of market research. Once we diagnose these crucial moments and their causes, we can begin to do something about it – just as Staci and her team did.

In 2020, more than 10 percent of shelters in the United States offer pet refuges – up from 4 percent just three years prior. Despite this success, Staci assures us that she is not done. Noah's has effectively "open-sourced" its procedures and operational models, providing free resources and advice so that any shelter in the country can create a similar model. She, in other words, has reduced the Effort of building pet-friendly shelters by giving people a clear *roadmap* to action. "My goal is to remove all the 'No pets allowed' signs on domestic violence shelter doors," she said. The way things are going, she just might.

The Emotional Life of Procurement

Staci Alonso instigated a nationwide movement because she found and removed the emotional roadblock that stood in the way of women getting the help they needed. But when it comes to Emotional Friction, innovators can also be the accidental antagonists in their own story.

A couple of years ago, David was invited to speak at the signature annual event for the world's top chief procurement officers (CPOs), in what was billed to him as (no joke), "The Davos of Procurement." The analogy alone made this invitation irresistible. A procurement officer is the person inside large organizations responsible for helping select and manage outside vendors and negotiate their fees. With their reputation for heavy-handed negotiation tactics and a relentless focus on cost-reduction, procurement officers are often viewed as adversaries, both inside and outside their organization. In actuality, procurement departments can be incredibly rich sources of ideas about organizational innovation.

After his presentation, David was sitting around the lunch table with CPOs from some of the largest companies in the world. It was clear from the conversation that most procurement officers had very similar goals and objectives: to enable their company to operate and grow its business while keeping costs as low as possible.

David asked one CPO from a major international bank for his reaction to the following idea: "Since your goals are to keep costs as low as possible, would your ideal scenario be that vendors show up on day 1 of the sales process with 'best and final' pricing? Would that make your department's job easier?" The answer from the bank CPO was an emphatic "No way!"

He went on to explain (off the record) that if every vendor showed up with best-and-final pricing, he worried that he and his department would be seen as unnecessary. To him, the *ideal* interactions with vendors resulted in "discovering" savings during the negotiation. This way, he and his team could confidently demonstrate to senior leaders their tangible value to the bank. Delivering this "emotional value proposition" of *feeling essential* to the success of the company was a key factor in the decision-making process of this CPO and, by extension, his entire organization.

David's suggestion inadvertently mutated a functional value into a challenging Emotional Friction. While he believed he was helping to save the procurement department time and Effort, he actually created anxiety and fear around their role in the company. After all, feeling obsolete is quite literally the opposite of feeling essential.

This example raises another important point. We often classify businesses into one of two *species*:

Business-to-consumer (B2C). Business models in which a company markets its offer directly to consumers (e.g., retail, consumer technology, social media).

Business-to-business (B2B). Business models in which a company
markets its offer to other companies (e.g., enterprise software, professional services, raw materials).

It can be easy to overlook the Human Element when it comes to
B2B business models. You are, after all, selling to a company, not an
individual. But as the procurement example highlights, businesses are
made up of many different individual "customers," each seeking their
own social, functional, and emotional value from the idea you are you
presenting.

Picking Second Best

Sometimes the value employees seek is perfectly in line with the company's goals. Sometimes it isn't. In either case, it serves innovators and
change agents well to invest a bit of time in understanding the many
different "jobs" that organizations and the individuals within them
are seeking to get done. Where there is clear tension between the two,
the perfect growing conditions exist for Emotional Friction. Hiring
decisions are a case in point.

Who would you rather hire, a stellar job candidate or someone
who is good-but-not-great? Sounds like a dumb question. Unfortunately, it isn't. It turns outs that leaders in companies routinely (and
deliberately) sabotage their teams by sidelining top performers.

Psychologists Charlie Case and Jon Maner designed a series
of experiments[5] that asked leaders to assign people to one of two
roles: a second-in-command position that was key to the success of
the team and an operational role that was less central to the team's
performance. The candidates varied in ability and track record. In
each experiment, there was a high-flying candidate with exceptional
credentials who was the obvious choice for the second-in-command

position. Yet Case and Maner found that leaders would often steer the stellar candidates away from the most influential roles.

In subsequent experiments, they found that leaders would undermine high-performing employees in other ways. Leaders often sidelined top performers by refusing to share important information with them. Leaders even took steps to isolate high performers by giving them roles that would prevent them from bonding with the team. Why would leaders do this? Chimpanzee behavior provides some insight. Chimpanzees at the top of the hierarchy are often quite supportive and caring of the other chimps in their troop. But there's one exception – the betas. These are members of the group who might be powerful enough to one day challenge the alpha's authority. Alpha chimps are notoriously hostile toward beta chimps because they are perceived as a threat.

The same is true for human leadership. In Case and Maner's experiments, the leaders often demoted the stellar candidates because they felt threatened by them. Most leaders enjoy having power and influence. Putting a high-flying candidate in an influential role might be best for the team but it also turns that candidate into a potential rival.

In theory, everyone in the organization should be rooting for and enabling the success of their colleagues, recognizing that this success lifts the entire organization. When Emotional Friction gets factored in, we learn a different truth.

The Shift to Self-Service Fuel

In 1947, a new epoch in American car ownership began. It was in this year that Los Angeles gas station owner Frank Ulrich opened the country's very first *self-service* filling station. Prior to this moment, all gas was pumped into cars and trucks exclusively by trained professionals. Cars would pull into a drive-through service station, a bell would ring, and out would come a uniformed employee ready to pump fuel into your tank, check your oil, top off the air in your tires, and clean your windows. These fueling specialists knew exactly what your car needed and when. The consumer did not need to lift a finger to have their needs met. It was, as the industry would later brand it, *a full-service* experience.

And this is how it worked for 40-plus years. There was no need for a consumer to learn anything about the process of fueling or what was going on under the hood of their car. All consumers needed to do was consume. The rest was taken care of by the pros.

Frank Ulrich saw the world differently. He believed that American consumers were quite capable of pumping their own fuel, and many would gladly do so if it meant saving a bit of money. So Ulrich began offering an innovation at his Los Angeles area filling stations that he called "self-service" fuel. Ulrich's slogan captured the value proposition clearly: "Save five cents, serve yourself, why pay more?" His idea caught on quickly. As do-it-yourself fueling stations proliferated around the country, it became clear that the way American drivers accessed fuel had permanently changed. The *self-service* era had begun. We have entered a similar era of "self-service" when it comes to accessing the Fuel that propels products, services, and ideas.[6]

When Ernest Dichter and his compatriots were laying the groundwork for emotional value, information about new products and services was dispatched to the public through ads in the newspaper and on radio and television. People relied almost entirely on the content of these fuel-sources and the feedback of their immediate social circles to make their purchasing decisions. There was no easy way to access information on new products and services on one's own, and as a result, ad content and sales pitches needed to be very rich in the "Ps" of Fuel and *pumped* directly to the customer by trained professionals. Marketing, sales, and persuasion were, in essence, *full-service* operations.

While companies still use advertising and sales presentations to communicate value, people today are far less reliant on these full-service channels than when Ernest Dichter was connecting your purchase of a pack of gum to your childhood relationship with your parents. Today's consumers are more empowered than ever to discover and learn on their own. Information on products, services, companies, and individuals is abundant (perhaps even *overly* abundant), and as a result, accessing "fuel" is far more of a *self-service* operation. As consumers, we know exactly where to go to gain the knowledge and data we need to make our decisions. Often, the source is no further than a device in our coat pocket or handbag. We live in a world where we now get to choose which ads we consume and fast-forward the ones we don't care to see. In fact, there are now businesses built around helping us *avoid entirely* traditional sources of full-service-marketing. Satellite radio, Spotify, and streaming television subscribers pay a premium to avoid consuming "pumped" ads.

Because of this shift to self-service Fuel, much of the magnetism we feel for new offers today is, to an extent, self-generated. We recognize that there is a problem we need to solve. We then head straight to the internet to consider our options. We compare the choices that we uncover. We might socialize our idea a bit with friends, colleagues, and extended networks (often online), and then, based on our individual scorecard of functional, social, and emotional value, we make a choice. By investing this time, we expect that the value we experience will exceed the energy required to achieve it – just like Frank Ulrich envisioned with the first DIY gas pump in the 1940s.

But there is a funky side-effect of self-service Fuel – it heightens the emotional risk of making the wrong choice. While people today are empowered to independently source their own data, the responsibility they feel in making these decisions can create Emotional Friction. The symptoms of the Emotional Friction caused by self-service Fuel are all around us. We procrastinate, hesitate, and consternate when making choices. We do more research on something *after* we buy it than before we buy it. We fill our online carts with goods, only to abandon them during the checkout process. As our society continues to evolve from full-service to self-service, the role of the innovator needs to evolve as well. As emotional risk grows, innovators must transition from being generators of demand to creators of individual confidence.

8 ♡ Overcoming Emotion

How to Quiet the Fears That Impede Progress

In a series of studies in the late 1990s and 2000s, a team of psychologists wanted to understand just how closely we pay attention to the world around us. In particular, they wanted to know how easily and often we spot anomalies in our environment. To answer these questions, the researchers focused on a group of people who pay attention to detail for a living – radiologists. Radiologists are responsible for reading and interpreting medical images (e.g., CT scans, MRIs, X-rays, ultrasounds, etc.). These doctors are rigorously trained in human anatomy, and it is their job to spot anything that is out of the ordinary in the images they examine.

The research team asked a group of radiologists to evaluate chest X-rays from routine physical exams. But the X-rays weren't really routine. Each image was altered so that the patient's collarbone was completely missing. If anyone is going to notice something strange on an X-ray, it is a radiologist. They are trained to spot hairline fractures. Surely experienced radiologists would be quick to notice that an entire bone was missing. Yet over 60 percent of the radiologists failed to spot the problem.[1]

On the chance that this study was a fluke, it was later followed up with another cohort of radiologists who had an average of over 15 years of clinical experience. This time they were given CT images of lung scans. The radiologists in this group were asked to search for nodules or masses in the lung scans. This time, instead of removing a key part of the patient's anatomy, the researchers inserted a picture of – get this – a gorilla angrily shaking its fists. A whopping 83 percent of these experienced radiologists failed to notice the gorilla (a gorilla!) in the images. In case you are wondering whether the image was too small to detect, the gorilla was *48 times larger* than an average lung nodule![2] What is going on here?

The reason radiologists didn't notice the gorillas was because they were, in a sense, unable to see them. Over the course of their training, radiologists develop a finely tuned mental model of what they expect to see in an X-ray. They are conditioned to spot anomalies consistent with *anticipated* human physiology, but are blind to phenomena that does not fit that preexisting mindset. Missing collarbones and threatening gorillas aren't noticed because radiologists are looking for something else.

This phenomenon of not seeing what we are not looking for is called *inattentional blindness*, and we experience it every day. Think about your last trip to the grocery store. During your mission to hunt down specific items, how attuned were you to the tens of thousands of other products on the shelves that weren't on your shopping list? Probably not much at all. Because you weren't looking for them, you didn't notice them. They did not fit the mental model of your shopping trip, so they hid in plain sight. The same is true with Emotional Friction.

Activating Latent Demand

But we *should* take notice. Addressing Emotional Friction isn't simply about removing a few hiccups from an idea to help it function a little better. Incredible opportunity awaits those who spot the frictions others have missed.

Think back to the Tinder example. Tinder was designed to remove the fear of rejection that was built into traditional dating websites. Removing the fear from the experience didn't just drag existing Match.com users over to Tinder. The far bigger impact is that it pulled in people who were sitting on the sidelines. It turns out that there was a huge pool of potential daters who liked the idea of meeting people through websites and apps, but the Effort and Emotional Friction of the Match.com-style sites held them back. Once those barriers were removed, the market exploded. Removing Emotional Friction from our innovations has many benefits. The most exciting is that doing so can dramatically *expand* the market for our ideas. There are countless examples like this.

Sweetwater Sound is a musical instrument and audio store based in Fort Wayne, Indiana. Like a lot of great companies, Sweetwater Sound has a heart-warming origin story. The company was founded in 1979 by Chuck Surack, a then 22-year-old musician who'd spent years touring the country as a saxophonist. Fatigued from his time on the road, Chuck longed to find a way to stay active in the music business while remaining closer to his Indiana home.

During his time as a touring musician, Chuck spotted an unmet need in the recording industry. He noticed that a lot of amateur musicians, from garage bands to church choirs, wanted to have their music professionally recorded. But traditional recording studios were costly and hard to come by outside of major cities. Chuck outfitted his hand-me-down Volkswagen minibus with recording equipment, transforming it into a mobile studio.

The business model was simple. He would drive to a church, school, or other venues and record live acts from the bus. He'd then convert the recordings into cassettes and sell them back to his clients, sometimes adding tracks that would include other instruments to enhance the professional quality of the music. That Volkswagen bus was the starting point for Sweetwater Sound.

Today, Sweetwater Sound is the largest online retailer of musical instruments and audio equipment in the United States. The company ships approximately 3,300 guitars, 37,000 guitar picks, 830 keyboards, 460 drum kits, and 5,300 microphones – every week. The success of Sweetwater is all the more remarkable when you consider that the past 20 years has been very hard on the musical instrument industry. Most of the piano, drum, and guitar stores have closed their doors. But while their largest competitor, Guitar Center, filed for Chapter 11 bankruptcy protection in late 2020, Sweetwater was having the best year in company history.

Much of Sweetwater's success comes down to mastering an Emotional Friction that their competitors missed. Guitar shops and other instrument stores are notoriously intimidating for beginners. These stores generally hire employees who are extremely knowledgeable about music and musical equipment. While a passion for making music is certainly a good thing, their expertise can be so superior that they can find it frustrating and downright boring to talk to a novice about the basics of instruments (sometimes referred to as the *curse of knowledge*). This frustration is often worn on their sleeves when interacting with brand new players.

Trying something new, whether it's playing a musical instrument, learning an unfamiliar sport, or speaking a new language, requires courage. Beginners fear feeling embarrassed by their lack of knowledge and ability. They fear being judged by others. In psychology, beginner anxiety is referred to as *the shame of the uninitiated*. This is often encapsulated in the anxiety the novice feels walking into a music store for the very first time – not knowing how to get started or what questions to ask. What a novice is *hoping* to hear at this moment are patient words of encouragement to help them through the first awkward months of learning. While this is the hope, the insider jargon and advanced terminology used by store employees delivers the opposite emotional experience. It signals – you don't belong here.

Because Chuck Surack got his start helping amateur musicians, he deeply understood the novice's anxiety. He realized that there were scores of people out there who have always *wanted* to learn to play an instrument, or to pick one up again after a long hiatus, but the uncertainty they felt kept them from turning aspiration into action. Sweetwater decided to deliberately design a sales culture that made all musicians feel comfortable – novice and expert alike.

To instill these values, every new Sweetwater employee must go through 13 weeks of training at *Sweetwater University* before they are ever allowed to interact with a customer. A big emphasis of the training is how to empathize and offer affirmation to a novice. Brandt Miller, a Sweetwater sales engineer shared:

> *When we first speak to a new client, we don't mention anything about gear. Guitars, amps, and drums may be the thing they are coming to buy, but before we start talking about equipment, I want them to fast-forward me to the end of the movie. What's their dream? What do they picture themselves doing in their mind's eye? Sometimes it's just about helping them choose the right piece of equipment or staying within a certain budget. But with beginners it's usually about having someone genuinely support their vision, encourage them that they can do it, and celebrate their willingness to take the first step in the journey.*

Sweetwater, in other words, celebrates the beginner. In this moment of validation, a critical layer of doubt is removed. The novice is no longer made to feel like an imposter. Instead, the novice begins to feel like a budding musician – which is the "job" they hired Sweetwater to do.

Because of this deliberate focus on empathy for beginners, Sweetwater attributes 30 percent of its year-over-year growth to new customers. Of that 30 percent, the company estimates that roughly half are new players, buying their very first instrument. These individuals wouldn't show up in industry reports and datasets surveying the musical instrument market because, prior to finding Sweetwater, they would never have considered themselves to be "musicians." Removing the intimidation from the experience allowed Sweetwater Sound to expand the market by turning *potential* musicians into active ones.

Overcoming Our Blindness to Emotional Friction

The first step to spotting Emotional Friction is to start looking for it. Our Fuel-based mindset means that Frictions aren't a natural part of our mental model (just like gorillas on lung scans). To begin seeing the Frictions that hold our ideas back, we need to start noticing them.

Unfortunately, Emotional Friction can be tricky to observe because most individuals tend to keep negative emotions hidden, especially when interacting with new ideas and new people. They rarely express their authentic feelings of worry or hesitation with clear, introspective language like, "This idea offends me," or, "Using this new product gives me anxiety," or, "Our company's newest hire makes me feel insecure." Instead of seeing the true negative emotions our ideas provoke in others, what we often observe are the *symptoms* of these underlying feelings – symptoms that may confuse or even belie the true problem. Sometimes a customer's "anxiety" expresses itself as "disinterest." Sometimes a colleague's "anger" shows up as "apathy." If we were to only treat the symptoms of these Emotional Frictions, we would not be able to overcome the cause of someone's resistance.

What we need are methods that can help us spot moments of Emotional Friction in the wild so that we might reframe them as opportunities for innovation. There are a number of techniques for uncovering Emotional Friction. Here we share three go-to approaches for detecting the emotional barriers that stand in the way of innovation.

Focus on Why

In 1978, the countries of Egypt and Israel traveled to Camp David in Maryland with the dim hope of reconciling 40 years of conflict. Each side had a long list of grievances, but the central issue was control over the Sinai Peninsula. Originally Egyptian land, Israel had gained control over the Sinai during the Six-Day War of 1967. Egypt wanted that land returned. Israel insisted on keeping it. The Camp David summit was a last-ditch Effort to find common ground between these two historic rivals. American negotiators worked tirelessly to find some mechanism of dividing the land in such a way that would be acceptable to both countries. But each time a map showing possible boundary lines was drawn, it would be immediately rejected. Volunteering to give up even one inch of the Sinai was totally unacceptable to Egypt. From their perspective, this was sovereign land that had belonged to Egypt since the time of the Pharaohs. But giving the land back was equally unacceptable to Israel. The countries remained deadlocked and further conflict seemed inevitable.

But then the negotiation team changed their approach. Instead of focusing on *what* they wanted they focused on *why* they wanted it. Israel's motivation was security. If they returned the land to Israel, Egyptian troops would be at their border, leaving Israel vulnerable to attack. Egypt had a completely different motivation. Its motivation was a desire to restore cultural pride and identity. For centuries, the Sinai had been occupied by foreign invaders. From the Roman to the British Empires, the Sinai had been outside Egypt's control. Egypt had only recently regained control of the land before the Six-Day War. Losing it yet again was unthinkable.

Prior to the Camp David summit, negotiations had centered on the functional aspects of the dispute (hectares of land, lines and borders). Once the conversation shifted from dividing the territory to the underlying reasons why they wanted the territory, a solution presented itself. The land would be returned to Egypt, but Egypt would agree to demilitarize the land. This solution removed the Emotional Friction that had previously stalled any attempts at progress.

In negotiation, reconciling conflict often comes from moving past people's positions (what they say they want) and focusing instead on their needs and interests (why they want it). Demanding territory be returned to you is a position. Asking for a raise is a position. Telling your suppliers they must reduce their price is a position. The reason why you want new territory, a higher salary, or reduced price is the motivating interest.

You can think about innovation as a negotiation between the innovator and the audience. When the audience resists or flat-out rejects a new idea, "no" is their position. It is the stated claim. But "no" doesn't tell us anything about the reason why they are resistant to change. To uncover the true reasons for resistance, we have to understand why. Understanding why is essential for diagnosing Emotional Friction. Think back to the Army recruiting example shared in Chapter 2. Resolving the Friction that keeps Army recruits who want to sign up but don't, can only happen if you understand what is holding them back (fear of having a difficult conversation).

Imagine that you are an entrepreneur attempting to promote new software that helps corporations better manage their social media feeds. After a sales presentation, a potential client tells you, "The software is certainly impressive, and I can see how it could make our lives easier, but you know . . . it's just too expensive for us."

Chances are you would interpret this feedback quite literally and respond with a Fuel-based conversation about budgets, value, payment plans, and ROI in hopes of overcoming the customer's objection. But, in reality, it's usually not about *cost*. The cost objection is often the fastest way for a customer to end a sales conversation and the easiest way of expressing overall doubt. What "cost" and "expense" frequently represent is a bundle of Frictions packaged together in a nice, neat word. The cost objection is a *symptom* of Friction, not the underlying cause. The key to identifying the root of the cost objection is taking the time to unpack the answer to get to the "why" underneath.

This method of digging deeper in business discussions was initially popularized as part of the *Toyota Production System* in the 1970s. To identify the cause of manufacturing problems before they grew, the company implemented a method called the *five whys*. The foundational premise is that the exact cause of any systemic manufacturing problem is typically five layers beneath the presenting symptoms. To arrive at the *true* source of a problem (or the underlying Friction) engineers would ask "why" five times during an investigation, and in doing so, the cause will be revealed.[3]

This method of questioning can be applied to uncover the root cause of any of the four Frictions, but is particularly good at spotting emotional resistance. For the entrepreneur who meets with opposition after the pitch, identifying the true reason for resistance to the new software might look something like this:

Customer. "The software is certainly impressive, and I can see how it could make our lives easier, but you know . . . it's just too expensive."

Entrepreneur. "I see. Help me understand a bit more about where you are coming from. Can you share a little more about your expectations around price, and what it is about the platform that causes you to think twice?" (Why #1)

Customer. "We knew it wouldn't be cheap, but I am just not sure that now is the time for us to invest in a new platform. We are right in the middle of end-of-year planning and most of our focus is on that at the moment."

Entrepreneur. "Got it. So, is it that the software is right, but the timing is not, or is there another factor at play as well?" (Why #2)

Customer. "Partly timing. It's also expensive enough that I would need board approval before I could proceed."

Entrepreneur. "How tricky is it to get the board to support a purchase like this? Sounds like maybe you have done this before. What was your last experience like?" (Why #3)

Customer. "Brutal. It took a ton of patience to champion the process, and the board really scrutinized the deal in ways I would not have expected. I did not really feel like we were on the same side. We got it through, but it was a very frustrating experience for me."

Entrepreneur. "I can imagine. Do you recall which components of the last initiative received the most scrutiny? Was it anything in particular?" (Why #4)

Customer. "They seemed to get hung-up on data privacy. I guess one of the board members had a pretty negative experience with this issue at her own company in the past and now she is extremely cautious with any decisions about software."

Entrepreneur. "Do you remember how you were able to address the concerns and move them past the problem?" (Why #5)

Customer. "Testimonials and references from other companies that the board admired helped calm them down. Once they knew that others they respected were using the platform successfully, they became much more comfortable."

When our audience voices an objection to a new idea, the *real* reason is several layers deeper than the original answer. To find it, innovators need to unpack the answer by asking "why" in various forms. While cost was a part of the story, it was not the root cause of the objection. The pivotal Friction was anticipated frustration – the worry that getting the board's buy-in would be difficult and tedious.

Identifying the core issue transforms the scenario. Knowing that these Emotional Frictions exist, the entrepreneur could help the customer to champion the process internally by creating presentation materials that include customer testimonials and outcome data from well-known organizations that currently use the software. Or the entrepreneur might commission a third-party data privacy audit of the platform as a condition of a successfully executed sale. Once we are clear on why Emotional Friction exists, we can begin to address removing the friction itself instead of treating its symptoms.

You may have noticed in the example above that discovering the true Emotional Friction did not involve the literal use of the word *why* in the question. Questions that reveal why people are resistant to new ideas tend to have three features:

1. *Ask open questions.* A closed question prompts a brief yes or no answer: "Is price important to your company?" If the entrepreneur asked this question, the client would simply say "yes." This would just reinforce the price objection and reveal nothing about the true underlying reasons. Open questions don't lend themselves to one-word answers and are therefore much better at revealing information. "Can you share a little more about your expectations around price, and what it is about the platform that causes you to think twice?" Asking the question in this way gets people talking.

2. *Ask probing questions.* People are often reluctant to reveal their fears and anxieties. Probing questions ask people to dig deeper into the issue. "What was your last experience like?" subtly nudges people to say more. Asking probing

(*continued*)

questions doesn't have to be complicated. The simple
phrase "that's interesting – can you tell me more?" works
great in most situations.

3. *Ask illuminating questions.* Illuminating questions focus
on how the new idea might conflict with one's needs or
objectives. "What is it about the platform that causes you
to think twice?" is very much an illuminating question.
Questions like these help you to discover what it is about
the new idea that people find threatening. By asking,
"Do you recall which components of the last initiative
received the most scrutiny?" we learn that worry over
data privacy is the true issue – and we get strong clues
about how to prevent this Friction in the future.

Become an Ethnographer

As famed entrepreneur and creator of the lean startup movement
Steve Blank is known for saying, "There are no facts inside of your
office, so get the heck outside." What people *show* you in the wild is
often far more powerful than what they *tell* you in a boardroom or
over a phone call.

An ethnographer is someone who studies users in their natural
habitat, such as their home or office. Shadowing others "in the wild"
helps ethnographers see the world as users do and provides insight
into how they actually behave without the editorial (and often misleading) filter of focus groups and other traditional market research
methods. Ethnography can give you a vital window into the unstated
needs and concerns of your audience and help you to anticipate
important Frictions before they arise.

Pay It, Plan It

In 2015, American Express noticed a worrying gap in its customer base. While Amex had long been the card of choice for older, more affluent consumers, its products had not gained much traction with younger audiences. In order to position itself for long-term success, American Express would need to appeal to the next generation – the millions of millennials who were beginning to use credit cards. But with dozens of credit card companies promoting the latest and greatest in rewards and perks, how would American Express stand out?

According to Kyoko King, VP of Global Commercial Services at American Express, "It felt like a race to the bottom. We kept throwing more rewards at the customer. So they win out, but there is no actual edge. That was the challenge we set out to solve."[4]

In order to better understand the needs of younger consumers, Amex, along with a team of designers from global design firm IDEO, went out into the field to observe how millennial consumers use credit cards to make purchases. As part of the research process, the team asked millennials to talk through the contents of their wallets and the financial apps on their smartphones. The team then asked them to explain the role each form of payment played in their financial lives. What quickly became apparent was that, in the minds of younger consumers, each form of payment did a very different job.

Cash was typically used for smaller purchases like cups of coffee or buying lunch at work. Debit cards were often used for purchases that exceeded the amount of cash someone happened to have in their pockets. Only the very large purchases were made using traditional credit cards.

This was a puzzling observation. After all, one of the primary benefits of most credit cards is that they reward customers for every dollar they spend. Why use cash to make a purchase at Starbucks when you could be earning 3 percent cash back on your latte or 12 hotel points toward your next vacation? The answer, it turned out, was Emotional Friction.

A major benefit of credit cards is that using them allows consumers to buy goods and services immediately and pay for them later, earning valuable rewards in the process. This works great for credit card users who are confident in managing their personal finances. But it also creates the temptation and risk to overspend.

Millennials grew up hearing stories about how credit cards ruined people's lives. They've heard this story so often, in fact, that many millennials have become frightened to use a credit card for everyday purchases. They have fear they might lose track of their spending, and have anxiety about how long it might take to pay off a credit card bill if they don't pay their statement in full each month. Credit cards, in other words, make millennials feel nervous. As one customer put it, "Why should I risk going into debt over buying a cup of coffee?" Another shared his terror every time a statement was delivered – an experience he referred to as "statement shock." To alleviate his monthly anxiety, he created his own remedy – proactively making multiple small payments before each billing cycle closed to diminish the size of his running balance. He had, in essence, "hacked" a solution to address the anxiety of using credit cards. This self-designed *workaround* made him feel like *he* was in control – not the credit card company.

Based on these insights, the American Express team arrived at a big idea. Rather than trying to attract younger customers with yet another credit card laden with more points and perks, why not offer them a card specifically designed to alleviate their anxiety about using credit cards in the first place. A card that instead of *creating* Emotional Friction, *removes* it. Taking inspiration from some of the home-grown solutions discovered during the ethnographic research (such as the clever micro-payment workaround mentioned above), the team created a new feature for American Express credit cards called *Pay It, Plan It.*

Pay It, Plan It empowers American Express customers to determine, on a purchase-by-purchase basis, which expenses they wish to pay-in-full at the end of each billing cycle and which they would like to finance over time. A cup of coffee at Starbucks or a new shirt at a retail store, for example, might be something a customer would choose to "pay" for – just as they would if they were using cash or a debit card. An emergency vet bill for an injured dog, on the other hand, might be the type of large, unforeseen expense that a card member chooses to "plan." When the "Plan It" feature is selected for a given purchase, the card member is immediately shown via the American Express app exactly what it will cost to finance that particular expense for a period of 3, 6, 12, or 18 months. This purchase-specific, fixed-fee financing model removes a huge amount of fear and anxiety younger consumers associate with the ambiguity of traditional credit cards.

What was meant to be a project aimed at attracting millennials to Amex quickly transformed into a Friction-reducing feature that is now included on *all* American Express credit cards. Since its launch in 2017, Pay It, Plan It has been used to create five million payment plans totaling nearly $4 billion in lending for American Express.

The Mindset of an Ethnographer

When performing ethnographic research, having the right "mindset" is critical. Here we offer three recommendations for approaching your ethnographic research with the right frame of mind.

Have a Progress Orientation

Many organizations confuse the "business" they are in with the products, services, and ideas they promote. An organization's value proposition is not what it sells, but rather, the

(continued)

progress (functional, social, and emotional) that it helps others make. This *progress orientation* is crucial to identifying and addressing Friction. Crucial because many of the Frictions that stifle innovation and change aren't product centered. For Beach House, the reason many customers disappeared right before clicking the "purchase" button had nothing to do with the product. A product orientation can only imagine product-based Frictions. An innovator with a product orientation widens the scope of consideration. It puts the innovation in a broader context. And it is in this broader context where the most powerful Frictions dwell.

Leave Your Biases at the Door

Understanding someone else's point-of-view is easier said than done. One way to do this is by taking inventory of the biases and beliefs that might muddle your interpretation of what you observe. These biases include things like the age, socioeconomic background, or political views of your team members – anything that you suspect *might* impact how you interpret the beliefs and behavior of those you seek to understand. Check in on your bias inventory from time to time and ask, "Might any of these factors be unfairly influencing what we are learning? If so, how might we adjust our approach?"

Reserve Judgment of Others

When performing ethnographic research, you will occasionally notice people having emotional reactions to things that don't make sense to you. It's tempting to dismiss people who don't meet our expectations. We say things like, "I can't believe she is reacting this way! She doesn't get it." "It's ridiculous that he's so worried about one small detail. Can't he see the bigger picture and get past it?" These reactions are part of human nature. But the moment you conclude that the people you are trying to influence are irrational or "nuts," you've lost. The denial of other people's feelings is the death of empathy. Instead, try your best to understand what might be happening through *their* eyes, as it's *their* lived experience that we are striving to understand.

Bring the Outside In

IDEO, the famed global design firm, got its start developing industrial and consumer products like the first Apple mouse. In the 40 years since its founding, IDEO has applied the practice of *design thinking* not just to the creation of products but to a wide variety of fields such as education, government, health care, and more.

The design industry is typically a young person's field, with many firms dominated by designers in their 20s and 30s. Youthfulness has its benefits. Looking at old problems through fresh eyes can be an asset in challenging the status quo. But it also presents a challenge. It requires designers to build products and services for users radically different from themselves.

This empathy rift can be particularly acute for projects focused on aging or elderly users. Despite their best efforts and intentions, it's difficult for a young designer to anticipate all the Friction an elderly user or a product will encounter, given it's not their lived experience. This is challenging enough when it comes to the functional facets of a product (screens, buttons, features, etc.), but it's even more challenging when it comes to anticipating the associated Emotional Friction.

In 2013, IDEO Founder David Kelley was featured on the popular CBS television show *60 Minutes* to talk about the evolution of design thinking and to share some of the key ingredients that lead to creative innovation. One of the principles Kelley mentioned was the importance of having diverse teams working on projects. One of the people watching this *60 Minutes* episode was Barbara Beskind, a retired designer living in the Bay Area, where IDEO's largest office is located. The *60 Minutes* segment provided an overview of design thinking, a method that uses the tools of design to solve problems and highlights the importance of being human-centered in the way new products and services are developed. Watching the segment inspired her to think that she would like to work at IDEO. "Oh, that sounds like it's for me," she remembers thinking.

Barbara decided to write a letter to IDEO expressing her interest in joining the firm. It didn't take the IDEO team long to appreciate the value that someone with Barbara's skills, experience, and perspective would bring to projects focused on aging. And just like that, IDEO had its newest designer onboard – at the spritely age of 90.[5]

Barbara's presence on project teams brought much-needed insight into how products might be designed to best serve other elderly users. This helped teams spot functional issues that young designers would often overlook – details like the size of buttons and user interfaces that might be challenging for those with arthritic hands or diminishing eyesight. Even more valuable was Barbara's ability to help teams anticipate the Emotional Frictions young designers couldn't forecast.

In one particularly poignant case, IDEO was approached by a company that owned and operated several senior living communities around the United States. The company wanted to update its marketing strategy to more directly appeal to the needs and desires of seniors. One idea they proposed was to ask new residents to pay an upfront activity fee of close to $3,000 – presumably to remove the hassle seniors might find in being charged for various activities on an a la carte basis.

When the team presented this business model feature to Barbara for her input, she was quick to point out a fundamental challenge with the Fuel-based pricing tactic:

> *It was very off-putting—quite insulting, in fact. What this company did not seem to understand is that for a senior forced to consider a move to an assisted living facility, everything in their life that has brought them to this moment has been a series of "losses." They have lost their house. They may have lost their spouse. They have lost their car, their mobility, their diet, they have undoubtedly lost some hearing and perhaps vision. This company did not realize that asking someone on a fixed income, who has just undergone a steady and emotional stream of losses, to make a large upfront payment of $3,000 for participating in community activities, shows a total lack of sensitivity to the journey that elder has been on. They would be better to just increase the monthly facility fee by $30 and bury the cost there. Asking someone to incur another big "loss" right up front (in the form of financial cost) at this moment in their life is just awful.*

Were it not for Barbara's voice, this source of Emotional Friction would not have been anticipated – at least not until poor sales data alerted the company to the problem. Insights like this one are not typically discovered through survey data or market research reports. Nor are they brought to light by spending a day shadowing an elderly potential customer. This type of insight can only be spotted by someone with deep *lived* experiences. That is why one of the best ways to generate empathy for those we wish to serve is to involve them in the innovation process itself. As Barbara Beskind puts it, when it comes to designing frictionless products and services for our elders, "It's far better to design *with* us than to design *for* us."

We call bringing the target audience into the innovation process *bringing the outside in.* The aim is to give the people you are trying to serve a seat at the table *during* the design process. Having your customers on your team can be the ultimate competitive advantage when it comes to creating offers with minimal Emotional Friction.

Hiring Your Customers

Livongo is one of the most impactful health care companies in the United States. Not only has it had a profound impact on the lives of its customers, but its success has also kickstarted a new era of digital medicine. Founded in 2014, Livongo's breakthrough technology was a blood glucose meter that automatically tracks and reports blood sugar readings, enabling users to better monitor and take control of their health. The Livongo glucometer also serves as a communication device. It provides members 24-hour access to a Certified Diabetes Educator (CDE) who can answer any questions they might have about living with diabetes and can coach them through adverse events they might encounter. Behind the scenes, the Livongo device keeps a careful eye on its members' health, scanning their blood sugar readings for any signals that might require proactive intervention from a CDE in order to prevent a particular hypoglycemic (low blood sugar) or hyperglycemic (high blood sugar) episode from getting out of hand. The stakes are high. A blood sugar episode that is left unmanaged can quickly turn fatal.

Chronic health conditions such as diabetes, hypertension, and heart disease are not just *functional* medical challenges. They are equally *emotional* challenges. These conditions and their symptoms are a constant source of anxiety for those that manage them. Livongo understands these emotional challenges because nearly half of the company's employees have chronic conditions like diabetes. Hiring people who know these challenges firsthand gives Livongo deep insight into its customers' needs and concerns, enabling the company to engage with its members far more empathically than other chronic disease management services. As Glen Tullman, Livongo's Founder and executive chairman, shared with us, "We know these conditions in ways that other people can't learn them."

One of the biggest emotional challenges for individuals with diabetes is dealing with other people's judgment. Dr. Jennifer Schneider, Livongo's President, a medical doctor, and herself a person living with Type 1 diabetes, explains that diabetes is a condition that elicits a lot of judgment and blame from those who are unfamiliar with it. In the case of people with Type 2 or later-onset diabetes, "There is a sentiment amongst the general public that these individuals did this to themselves through choosing poor diets, lacking exercise, or being overweight. For these individuals, this constant fear of being blamed by others really gets in the way of being open about their challenges and making progress against them," she told us.

Glen Tullman shared that when a typical diabetes service receives a call from a user in need of assistance with a hyperglycemic event, the first question they often hear from the person on the other end of the phone is, "Well, what did you have to eat?" "While that question is practical," Tullman said, "it strikes a tone of blame on the part of person with diabetes. It suggests that it was their fault, through their own choices, that they got themselves into this situation. The truth is that sometimes the human body just does some strange things and reacts to things in weird ways. So leading with this undertone of blame just makes an already bad moment even worse."

To counteract this Friction, Livongo has designed all of its interactions, from text messages to user interfaces to phone calls, to be completely free of language that implies blame. Livongo instead designs its interactions to focus on solving the problem at hand – not attributing responsibility for it. Instead of asking a question like, "What did you eat?" a Livongo coach will simply ask a member, "What do you need?" As Tullman puts it, "This makes it clear to the member that in this relationship we are working *for you*. We are not here to blame anyone for the challenging situation they find themselves in at a particular moment in time. We are here to empower them."

Livongo's deep understanding of the people they serve shows up in other important ways. "There are health care organizations out there that when they first learn one of their members has been diagnosed with diabetes, they will call that person and say, 'We are so sorry. We hear you have diabetes. We know that this disease can be very serious and lead to blindness and even amputation. We just want you to know that we are here for you,'" Tullman tells us. "That is the *opposite* of what someone wants to hear in that moment . . . This type of outreach tries to use empathy without a true and realistic understanding of what people need in that moment." In other words, its *empathy theater*. Empathy theater is manufactured sympathy designed to ease someone's concern. Anyone who has ever called their cable company with an issue to resolve knows exactly what empathy theater sounds like.

Livongo never uses words like *help*, *diabetic*, or *patient*, because these words make people feel helpless, sick, or otherwise defined by their condition. As Glen Tullman puts it, "You would never call someone battling cancer 'a cancer.' Why then would you call someone managing diabetes by the name of their disease? Words matter." Instead of *diabetic*, Livongo uses the language *people with diabetes*. To an outsider this might seem like a trivial distinction, but to someone living with a chronic illness, it matters a great deal.

These subtle but powerful insights come from having people with firsthand experience on the Livongo team. "We used to joke with our HR leader that we had an unusually high spend on our own employee health because we hired and attracted a lot of people with diabetes," said Dr. Schneider. "And that's actually a really great thing because at the end of the day you have to deeply understand what that experience is in order to remove the obstacles that stand in their way."

When we asked Dr. Schneider about the biggest difference between companies that "hire their customers" to build new ideas versus those that build ideas without direct experience she told us something very interesting: "Builders can get so consumed with the *thing* they are building that they lose touch with the needs and the anxieties of the people they are building it for. Once they have the idea, they tend to stop listening. When teams include the very people whose problems are being solved, that listening never stops." As a result, Emotional Friction is being constantly monitored and addressed in real time.

This heavy emphasis on hiring your customers seems to be working. In just four years, Livongo went from inception to going public on the NASDAQ, achieving a $4 billion valuation on its very first day of trading. In 2020, the company merged with telemedicine provider Teledoc in a deal that valued the combined enterprise at $18.5 billion. Despite its rapid growth, Livongo remains committed to finding innovative ways of removing Friction that stands in the way of people with chronic conditions living better and healthier lives.

Common Remedies for Emotional Friction

While selecting the appropriate remedy to quiet Emotional Friction depends on its underlying cause, there are three "greatest hits" approaches commonly used to ease user anxiety.

Allow for Trial

Free trials have long been used as a way of minimizing the Emotional Friction associated with trying something for the first time. Trials come in many forms, but the most commonly

(continued)

used are time-constrained sample periods before commitment
is required, such as a 30-day free trial of a subscription streaming service. A "Freemium" model is another example, whereby
a user can get started with a "basic" version of a product or
service at no cost, then upgrade to a more feature-rich paid
version once they feel confident in its value.

Make Decisions Easily Reversible

Emotional Friction is often born out of our fear that we
might commit to the wrong choice. Our anxiety is intensi-
fied when we worry that a decision is permanent. One way
to ease this discomfort is to make decisions easily reversible –
enabling users to quickly undo a choice they later have second
thoughts about. Common embodiments of this approach are
programs like "no hassle" return policies, money-back guarantees, and "cancel any time" contracts.

Include a Service Element

Even if your innovation happens to be a product, adding an
element of "service" to the offer can go a long way toward eas-
ing a new user's anxiety about committing to it. This is precisely the approach taken by Beach House when they decided
to include the removal a customer's existing sofa as part of the
purchase of a new one. This same method was implemented
by Apple when it established *Genius Bars* in all of its retail
stores and Best Buy's integration of the *Geek Squads*. Both services exist to help customers feel comfortable and confident in
using their new devices and by providing assurance that there
is always a human available to help them should anything go
wrong down the road.

Emotional Friction is the unintended negative feelings that inhibit a new idea or innovation. Even the most promising idea can unintentionally trigger negative emotions that become significant barriers to adoption. To determine the level of Emotional Friction that awaits your next idea, ask these two questions:

1. *To what extent might the audience feel threatened by or anxious about the proposed change?* The more fearful or anxious people are about a new idea, the stronger Emotional Friction will be.

2. *Does the innovation have the potential to undermine people's broader needs?* As the cake mix example demonstrates, increasing functional value can inadvertently threaten important emotional and social needs.

In order to address Emotional Friction, we first need to identify its source. This can be tricky because most individuals tend to keep the root causes of their negative emotions hidden from view. Once recognized, however, these Frictions can be alleviated, and the progress of innovation can continue. This chapter explored three methods for detecting Emotional Friction in the wild: *focus on why, become an ethnographer, and bring the outside in*. These questions will help you spot, diagnose, and eliminate the Emotional Friction that impedes your most promising ideas.

Focus on Why

1. *Why are people "hiring" your innovation? What functional, social, and emotional value does your idea create?* It's important to remember that all three dimensions of value are present in every decision we make. Identifying the broader needs your innovation satisfies will help you spot the emotions that work against it.

2. *Are you focused on the symptoms of Emotional Friction or treating its underlying cause?* Think about innovation as a negotiation

between the innovator and the audience. When the audience resists or flat-out rejects a new idea, "no" is their position. It is the stated claim. But "no" doesn't tell us anything about the reason why they are resistant to change. "No" is a symptom of Friction. To uncover the true reasons for resistance, we have to understand why. The *five whys* interview method is one way to uncover the true reason people reject change.

3. *What business are you actually in?* Many organizations confuse the "business" they are in with the products, services, and ideas they promote. While indeed hardware stores sell hardware supplies and consultancies sell consulting services, in the customers' minds these products are merely means to achieving a larger goal. A *progress orientation* is crucial to identifying Emotional Friction because it puts the innovation in a broader context. And it is in this broader context where the most powerful Frictions dwell.

Become an Ethnographer

1. *How might observing someone's behavior enrich your understanding of their Emotional Friction?* People will often say one thing and do another. This tension makes it difficult to rely on conversation alone to identify true points of emotional resistance. Shadowing others "in the wild" can give you vital insight into the unspoken needs and concerns of your audience and help you to anticipate these Frictions before they arise.

2. *How well do you understand your audience's context?* Behavior doesn't happen in a vacuum; it happens in rich social, emotional, and physical contexts. Seeing people in their natural environment can give you deep insight into their needs and what trade-offs they are willing (and unwilling) to make in order to accomplish them.

3. *What solutions has your audience invented for themselves?* As we saw in the Pay It, Plan It example, people often create workarounds to address their Emotional Friction. Ethnography can help you spot them. Once identified, these workarounds are fantastic starting points for designing more elegant and frictionless solutions to meet your audiences' needs.

Bring the Outside In

1. *Is there an opportunity to bring your audience into the innovation process?* Having the people you serve actively participate in the innovation process gives you greater understanding of the concerns and anxieties likely to make them resistant to the change you are seeking.

2. *Can you hire your customers?* To ensure that your organization is continually innovating with empathy, consider making the people you serve permanent members of your team.

9 ⬡ Reactance

Why We Feel the Impulse to Resist Change

Few examples better capture the human mind's irrational resistance to change than the seat belt. Today in the US and much of the world, there is overwhelming support for the use of seat belts. Wearing a seat belt reduces your chance of dying in a car crash by nearly 50 percent and saves roughly 30,000 lives in the United States each year. It's a relatively pain-free precaution with undoubted benefits to personal and public health. Wearing a seat belt, in other words, is an unquestionably good idea.

But in the 1980s, Americans waged war against seat belts. The war began in 1984 when New York became the first state to make wearing a seat belt mandatory. A wave of states soon followed. But this well-intended policy produced public outrage. In defiance, some people cut the seat belts from their car. Others filed lawsuits against the new mandate. In Massachusetts, a group called the Crusade against Seat Belts gathered enough signatures to get a referendum on the ballot. As late as 1986, only 17 percent of Americans regularly wore a seat belt, and the vast majority objected to laws mandating their use. Widespread opposition to seat belt laws continued for another decade. In hindsight, the long road to seat belt adoption is a tragic story. The reluctance to change cost tens of thousands of lives.[1]

Fast-forward to 2020; this same story repeats itself. This time, the debate was over face mask requirements. Like seat belts, face masks were an easy and effective way to reduce a public harm – the spread of COVID-19. Yet many people refused to wear them. The public's reluctance to adopt these safety measures was truly puzzling. They reduced the spread of the virus at very little cost. Yet in much of the country, there was strong public and political opposition to making face masks mandatory.

Opposition to commonsense safety measures reveals a deep (and often disastrous) human tendency. People don't like having change imposed on them. We don't like being told what to do. This is a major obstacle for the innovator, because innovation is the act of changing what people do. This means that the innovator's objective is at odds with our human nature. And when people feel they are being pressured to change, the automatic reaction is to react *against* change. We call this tendency Reactance. Reactance leads us to see new ideas not as opportunities, but as invaders. So we raise the drawbridge and arm the gates. If Inertia is the resistance to change, Reactance is the resistance to *being* changed.

Rats, Graffiti, and the Origins of Reactance

To understand why humans act this way, we need to go back to 1971, when a psychologist by the name of Jay Weiss designed an ingenious experiment – an experiment that would, some years later, help him earn a MacArthur grant (aka the genius prize).[2] Dr. Weiss studies how animals cope with stress, and how features of the environment determine whether a stressful situation is manageable or overwhelming.

Imagine three lab rats, each living in a separate cage. Rat A is living the most perfectly normal lab rat life you can imagine – a small metal cage, a watering tube, and a routine feeding schedule. Rat B is living under the same conditions, with one important difference.

The floor of the metal cage is an electrified grid. At random intervals, the electricity turns on, delivering a painful but nonlethal shock. There is a small lever at the top of the cage. The rat instinctively reaches for the lever to pull itself from the painful floor. The moment the rat touches the lever, the electricity stops. It only takes a rat one or two trials to learn that when the electricity starts, simply push the lever. Rat C has the same electrified floor – but no lever. What determines when the electricity stops? Rat B. The electricity hits them both at the same time and stops for both when Rat B hits the button. Notice that both rats endure the identical amount of pain. What's the key difference? One has the ability to make it stop and the other doesn't. This is like desperately needing a promotion at work, but your evaluation isn't based on what you do but rather the person in the cubicle next to you.

Dr. Weiss then looked at the health of each rat. You do that by measuring whether or not they have ulcers. Stressed rats get a lot of them. Happy rats don't. Rat A, as you'd expect, was fine. Maybe a little bored, but minimal signs of stress. The real test was the health of Rats B and C. Turns out, Rat B looked similar to Rat A – a few ulcers, but nothing serious. Rats aren't exactly delicate flowers. They can handle some adversity. The shocks were painful but the rats could cope. Rat C was a different story. More than double the ulcers of Rat B. In other words, despite receiving the same amount of pain, the effect of that pain was more traumatic for the rat that didn't have autonomy of freedom over its environment.

This finding, believe it or not, can help us understand why humans experience Reactance. Like rats, humans have a fundamental need for freedom over their environment. Freedom is a basic human need because it is essential for survival. Freedom allows us to select options that are beneficial and desirable and avoid options and outcomes that are detrimental. The desire for freedom is so deeply ingrained, people prefer situations that give them freedom of choice, even when that choice affords no material benefits. In one experiment, people had to decide between two options. One option led to a second choice and the other did not. People instinctively preferred the option that leads to the second choice, even though the additional choice didn't carry any meaningful benefits and required more work.[3]

The trouble is, when we attempt to influence people we are, in effect, imposing on their freedom. We are attempting to push them down a particular path. When people feel their freedom being threatened, their instinct is to restore their freedom by pushing back.

Understanding that Reactance is rooted in the desire to protect our autonomy is a critical insight. It suggests that the more we feel our freedom is being taken, the more we will feel the need to push back. For example, to reduce graffiti in the men's bathroom, a university tested two different signs. One sign read, "Do not write on these walls under any circumstances." The other read, "Please don't write on these walls." A few weeks later they checked the results. Both messages backfired – the messages led to more graffiti than ever before (and, one suspects, with more vulgar messages too). But the bathrooms with the strongest message "Do not write on these walls under any circumstances" had the most graffiti by far. The stronger push created stronger push back.[4]

Why Strong Evidence Is the Worst Evidence

Innovators quickly learn to expect new ideas to be met by knee-jerk doubt and disapproval. When we encounter resistance to a new idea, the innovator's impulse is to add Fuel. We attempt to overcome resistance by igniting the idea with more evidence and encouragement. But there is a risk in this approach that innovators rarely consider. If our attempts to create change trigger Reactance, opposition to the innovation intensifies. This is what makes Reactance so dangerous to innovation. If, for example, you believe climate change is the biggest challenge facing humanity but the person across the table from you thinks it is a hoax, no amount of evidence will change her beliefs. Her mind will effortlessly discount or distort facts that you see as irrefutable. But by attempting to change her mind, you've likely made her more resistant to change.

To see how easily giving people evidence can backfire, consider this recent experiment.[5] Two hundred people who favored capital punishment (i.e., the death penalty) were recruited for an experiment. Half were given a research article that supported their beliefs. The article concluded that the death penalty was effective because it reduces crime. The other half read an article that conflicted with their death penalty beliefs – the article concluded that the death penalty wasn't an effective deterrent against crime. After reading the article, both groups' opinions on capital punishment were reassessed.

The researchers wanted to know, by the end of the experiment, which of these two groups would show the strongest support for the death penalty. The answer seems obvious. In a sensible world, seeing the pro-death data should have strengthened support for capital punishment and the anti-death penalty data should temper their views. But that's not what happened. As you would expect, reading about the benefits of capital punishment slightly strengthened their initial opinion. However, reading a conflicting message didn't weaken their position. Seeing evidence against the death penalty inexplicably strengthened their support for capital punishment. After seeing evidence that the death penalty didn't deter crime, the pro-death penalty group clutched on to their beliefs more tightly than before. Classic Reactance. When people felt pressured to change, their instinct was to close their minds and defend their beliefs.

When faced with evidence that conflicts with the way they see the world, people often prefer to reject the evidence rather than question their beliefs. But what if the evidence is undeniable? How far will people go to protect their belief system? To answer that question, a psychologist by the name of Leon Festinger decided to join a cult.

The year was 1953, and a cult called the Seekers made head-
lines for predicting that a flood was coming to destroy civilization.
The prophecy came from the group's founder, Dorothy Martin. She
claimed to communicate with an advanced race of beings from the
planet Clarion. They warned her of the coming flood and promised
to rescue the Seekers in a flying saucer before the great deluge. One
detail of the prophecy caught Festinger's attention: it was specific!
The group indicated the precise date and time of the flood. It was all
going to end on midnight, December 21, 1956.

Festinger wanted to know: how would these people react when
(presumably) the prophecy fails? When confronted with indisputable evidence, would they abandon their beliefs, turn on their leader,
maybe even have a good laugh? He joined the group to find out. Here
is a timeline of events, taken from Festinger's report of the experience
in his book, *When Prophecy Fails*:

- *6 p.m., December 20 (six hours until salvation). Dorothy receives a
  message from the Clarion race with instructions for final preparation.
  The group is told they cannot bring any metal objects with them on
  their space voyage. So the group removes all zippers and other metal
  pieces from their clothing. There's debate about whether bras and
  shoes have metal in the straps and heels. To be safe, it is determined
  shoes and bras should be left behind.*

- *12:00 a.m., December 21 (the moment of rapture). The group sits in
  complete silence waiting for a knock on the door.*

- *12:05 a.m., December 21. No visitor. Someone notices that
  another clock in the room shows 11:55. Relieved, they agree it is not
  yet midnight.*

- *12:10 a.m. The second clock strikes midnight. Still no visitor. The
  group sits in stunned silence.*

- *4:00 a.m. The group continues to sit in stunned silence. A few
  attempts at finding explanations have failed. Dorothy begins to cry.*

- *4:45 a.m. Another message is sent to Dorothy. It states, in effect, that the God of Earth has decided to spare the planet from destruction. The cataclysm has been called off: "The little group, sitting all night long, had spread so much light that God had saved the world from destruction."*

- *Afternoon, December 21. Newspapers are called; interviews are sought. The group begins an urgent campaign to notify the public that the Seekers had saved the world.*

Instead of admitting error and changing their beliefs, the Seekers found new evidence. Like the capital punishment experiment, presenting the Seekers with a conflicting point of view didn't convince them to change their beliefs or admit they were wrong. Instead, it strengthened their conviction.

Cults are an easy target. But their reaction is, in fact, an ordinary human response. Once a strong belief forms, people can be impervious to influence. Reactance blinds us to new ideas and information. For the innovator, this is no laughing matter. In Chapter 2, we explored some of the limitations of Fuel. Reactance highlights an additional shortcoming. What happens when we give facts to people who oppose our message? Fuel doesn't just fail to change their minds – it often intensifies their opposition.

Rethinking the Hard Sell

Reactance has important implications for how we pitch ideas and pursue change. Consider this puzzle. In an experiment by organizational psychologist Adam Grant, alumni of a university were sent an email seeking donations.[6] Alumni received one of three messages. One message appealed to altruism: "Giving is your chance to make a difference in the lives of students, faculty, and staff." Another appealed to self-interest: "Alumni report that giving makes them feel good." A third email used both messages. The results were counterintuitive. Both the altruistic and the egotistic messages in isolation were effective – they led to a small but meaningful increase in donation rates. But when the two were combined, the message backfired.

If adding one influence tactic to the message was effective, why would adding two backfire? You might predict instead that it would double the message effectiveness. It's because people who received both tactics were aware that the email was designed to persuade them. They reported feeling pressured by the message. The double-tactic email, in other words, triggered Reactance. And once that happened, their impulse and priority was to restore their sense of freedom, not give to charity.

What this study demonstrates is that Reactance isn't just triggered by the restriction of actual freedoms or options. Simply the feeling of being persuaded is enough to trigger resistance. This is precisely why people have trepidation walking into a car dealership. It's not that people fear the aggressive sales tactics will work on them – it is that the experience of being pressured and persuaded is unpleasant.

In the last decade, persuasion tactics (or nudges) like *social proof, scarcity,* and *decoy effects* have become widely used tools of the marketing trade. These tactics can, for very little cost, produce a significant shift in behavior. But consumers today are much more nudge-aware than they were a decade ago. As people become more aware of these tactics, the likelihood they will backfire grows. In one recent consumer study, shoppers were shown one of two clothing ads. The ads were identical except for one difference – one ad displayed the message "buy now, only three left in stock."[7] This is what we would call *faux-scarcity*. It is an Aversive Fuel designed to spur people into action. People who received that message were less likely to purchase the product and also reported forming negative feelings about the brand. Interestingly, the more people were "brand loyalists," the more they resented the message. The ad backfired because people saw through it, and their instinct was to push back against the overt manipulation.

A California energy company attempted to create a nudge to influence its customers to use less electricity. The company sent reports to its customers comparing their electricity use to the average consumer. Nudge psychology would predict that this comparison should reduce electricity use. The nudge was successful for politically liberal customers. But conservative customers felt manipulated by the message and rebelled against it by increasing their electricity consumption (and their monthly bill).[8]

Reactance Requirements

Not every situation is ripe for Reactance. There are many instances where people will readily follow orders rather than react against them. Reactance is strongest under three conditions.

When the Idea Threatens a Core Belief

If your idea touches on issues you avoid at the Thanksgiving table (politics, religion, social justice), it's probably a core belief. If your idea challenges one's identity, Reactance is going to be strong. Consider the Seekers, the cult that predicted the end of the world. Their beliefs came at a tremendous price – it cost them their credibility, their family, and their careers. It's hard to be open-minded about the possibility that your beliefs are wrong when you have sacrificed so much.

When People Feel Pressured to Change

When people feel pressured to change, their instinct is to push back in order to maintain their autonomy. Pressure comes in many forms.

Penalties and punishment for failing to change is one form. Penalties inspire rebellion. One recent study found that when taxpayers were threatened with harsher penalties for common tax evasion practices (e.g., reporting personal expenses as business expenses), the effort backfired: people were more inclined to hide taxable income.

Time is another form of pressure. People often need time to adjust to new ideas. They need time to think through the implications. An impatient, everybody-get-on-board mentality, can make people feel they are being asked to change before their questions and concerns have been answered.

The tone of the message can also be the culprit. Does the message feel like a command? Commands are strong Reactance generators. Remember the graffiti in the bathrooms example. "Under no circumstances should you write on the walls" backfired terribly. The worst strategy is an empty command. Never issue a command if you don't have the authority or ability to enforce it (like we've done in this sentence).

Finally, does the role or circumstance imply pressure? Do people, in other words, anticipate pressure? When you walk into a car dealership, you expect the hard sell. This is the principal Friction Ali Reza, the world champion car salesperson, must overcome.

When the Audience Has Been Excluded

Finally, we need to consider where the idea came from. Often, the idea comes from, and is fully developed by, the innovator. The customers or workers who must implement the change have no voice in the process. They are simply expected to execute. When people aren't involved in the design of an idea – when their opinion wasn't sought or heard – anticipate Reactance.

Quite the conundrum. The aim of innovation is to lead people to embrace new ideas. But if people feel pushed, their instinct is to push back against change. How do we possibly overcome this Friction? The answer: unlearn everything we know about influence.

10 ⬟ Overcoming Reactance

How to Help Your Audience Persuade Themselves

We recently gave people the words *influence* and *persuasion* and asked them to write down the first words that came to mind. The top three words were: *manipulate, convince,* and *sell.* People instinctively associate the act of influence with *imposing* their ideas onto others. But masters of influence know something that the rest of us don't. Pushing rarely works. The greater the push, the greater the Friction.

The secret to overcoming Reactance is to stop pushing for change. Rather than attempting to persuade others, we should help them to persuade themselves. We call this approach to influence and innovation, *self-persuasion.* Self-persuasion occurs when the arguments and insights for change come from within.

The Power of Self-Persuasion

The evidence for self-persuasion is clear and compelling. In one simple study, a group of smokers were divided into two conditions: speakers and listeners. Speakers were asked to read aloud an anti-smoking article to another smoker. Listeners heard the identical message, but it had been spoken to them by another smoker. Keep in mind that for both groups, the message was the same. For the speakers, at least in a superficial sense, the message came from them. They didn't write the words in the message but they were nevertheless speaking the message. For the listeners, the message was read by someone else (i.e., the message was told to them). The results showed that those who read the message aloud found the arguments more compelling and were more motivated to quit smoking compared to those who heard the identical message. Simply altering whether the source of the message came from within or from someone else impacted its persuasiveness.

The power of self-persuasion can also be seen in the context of drug addiction: 78 percent of Americans are affected by drug and alcohol addiction. Chances are, someone in your close circle of friends and family struggles with addiction. How would you convince them to seek treatment? You could take the emotional approach. You might plead with them in the hope that it triggers their guilt. "Think of what this is doing to not just you but your family," you might implore. Or maybe you focus on fear. You threaten to cut them out of your life if they don't change. Or maybe you take a more analytical approach, citing figures and statistics about the dangers of drug abuse. It doesn't matter, really, because all of these techniques share the same problem – you are *telling* them what to do. You are forcing a view onto them. You are explaining the risks of drug use and the benefits of sobriety (benefits they, by the way, understand perfectly well already). Not only will this approach not work, it will probably backfire, pushing addicts further from sobriety.

Addiction counselors have stumbled onto a better way. Rather than explaining the risks of addiction, or making them fearful of their future, addiction counselors often begin the meeting by asking an unexpected question:

Imagine a scale from 1 to 10. A "10" means you are completely committed, with no reservations, to a life of sobriety. You will be clean and sober from this moment forward. A "1" is the very opposite. You see no benefits to sober living. You have no reservations, no fear, and no concern about living the rest of your life as an addict. Where are you on this scale?

Every addict feels deep ambivalence about their addiction. The rational mind wants to change, but their urges hold them back. So addicts never answer "1" or "10." Most addicts answer somewhere between a "2" and "4" on this scale. And that's exactly the answer the counselor is looking for, because it leads to the critical, follow-up question: "Why aren't you a 1?" Giving an answer of "2" or "4" implies that you see some benefits to sobriety. Asking, "Why aren't you a 1?" is a question that prompts the addict to generate her own pro-sobriety arguments. Rather than trying to persuade the addict, the counselor is letting the addict persuade herself.

This example highlights the first rule of self-persuasion: ask rather than tell. Rather than telling people what to think, self-persuasion uses questions that lead to self-discovery. Let's looks at two more examples of the power of self-persuasion.

The Power of Notecards

Bob Ladouceur is a name you should know. ESPN crowned him "the greatest prep high school football coach of all time." His story is so remarkable that it was the subject of a major Hollywood movie, *The Game Stands Tall.*

Coach Lad led the De la Salle Spartans for three and a half decades. During that time, he amassed 20 perfect seasons and an unbelievable winning streak that lasted from 1992 to 2003. That's right. He went undefeated for an entire decade. In any industry, being the best is hard. But sustaining success is another matter entirely. How do you get a team of 17-year-olds to remain hungry and buy in to the idea of relentless excellence? For Coach Lad, a big part of the answer is the humble 3 × 5 notecard.

Before we say more about the secret of the notecard, a few observations. Bob Ladouceur doesn't have a radical message. He is asking his team to embrace the same ideals you would see in locker rooms across the country – accountability, putting the team first, etc. What sets him apart is how deeply he gets his players to commit to these ideals.

How does the typical coach inspire excellence? She likely follows what we might call the *inspirational leader* archetype. It's a leader who is relentless in the pursuit of winning. A leader who demands high standards and uses a mix of tough-talk and infectious enthusiasm to achieve it. We imagine the impassioned halftime speech that gets players to believe in themselves in a way they never did before. This, you might notice, is the classic view of how influence happens. The coach is the source of change. She *injects* passion and belief into her players.

You won't find Coach Lad in this stereotype. Perhaps his greatest instrument of influence and buy-in is a 3 × 5 notecard, which he and everyone else at the school calls commitment cards. Here's how it works. Each week, Coach Lad would pair two players together – a new pair each week. Players would write down a goal for the three phases of football: a conditioning goal (How will I get stronger?), a practice goal (What skill will I improve upon?), and a game goal (What am I going to achieve during the game?). At the end of each week, players would share their commitments and reflect on whether they had lived up to them. And if not, they ask themselves: Why not? And how will they be better next week?

Like the smokers reading the message themselves, success for the players came not from being inspired by the coach but by being inspired by themselves. The coach isn't telling them how to improve. Coach Lad designed a weekly ritual that encouraged the players themselves to commit to excellence. The most successful high school football coach in history was inspiring players by helping them to inspire themselves. The results on the field suggest that through *self-persuasion,* the team developed a deeper commitment to the mission than the competition.

The Coach Lad story is an inspiring example of the power of self-persuasion. But it comes with a caveat. The players and the coach were, from day 1, aligned in their goals. The players already wanted to win. He didn't have to persuade them of that.

Can self-persuasion still work when we are dealing with people who oppose our message, or is this just a technique for strengthening resolve? Not only does self-persuasion work against those who oppose our ideas, but self-persuasion is often the only thing that does.

Deep Canvassing

The Los Angeles–based Leadership Lab is a nonprofit organization that aims to reduce discrimination against the LGBTQ community, with a particular focus on transgender rights. Transgender rights is currently a battleground issue in the United States. Americans are fundamentally divided over whether it is possible for someone to be a gender different from the sex they were assigned at birth. According to a 2017 survey by the Pew Research Center, roughly half the population (54 percent) oppose transgender rights. And like most social issues in America, there is a deep political divide. Democrats overwhelmingly favor transgender rights and Republicans strongly oppose.[1]

David Fleischer, the founder of the Leadership Lab, created the organization to shift attitudes (and ultimately policy) on transgender rights. But how do you change such deeply held, oppositional attitudes? Enter *deep canvassing*, a new approach to door-to-door canvassing that would rightly be called revolutionary.

Deep canvassing is based on a simple idea: rather than tell voters what to think and how to vote, you need to ask the right questions. The basic sequence of a deep canvas interaction has five steps:

Step 1: Ask the voter to share an opinion on a particular issue.

Step 2: Probe their beliefs by asking them why they feel the way they do.

Step 3: Ask the voter to share a personal experience with the issue.

Step 4: Canvasser shares a personal story that empathizes with the voter's initial view.

Step 5: Ask again about their opinions on the issue.

In practice, a deep canvass interaction looks something like this: The conversation begins with the canvasser asking the voter for her opinion on an issue (e.g., transgender rights). As the voter shares her opinions, the canvasser listens carefully but withholds judgment – the canvasser shouldn't reveal whether she is happy or hurt by the response.

The canvasser then asks if the voter has a personal connection to this issue. She might ask the voter, for example, if family members or coworkers are transgender. The canvasser might at this point share her own personal experience with the issue. Finally, the voter is asked: "When was the last time someone showed you compassion when you really needed it?" This question is designed to get the voter to feel connected to people from a disadvantaged group. It helps voters come to the self-realization that they have shared humanity with people they may have previously seen as being very different from themselves.

Consider how different this is from traditional canvassing. Typically, an *activist* hits people over the head with a list of arguments about why the voter should support the cause and shames anyone who holds a different opinion. As Dave Fleischer said in a recent interview, "Instead of pelting voters with facts, we ask open-ended questions and then we listen. And then we continue to ask open-ended questions based on what they just told us. The idea is that people learn lessons more durably when they come to the conclusion themselves, not when someone slaps you with a statistic."

Who is targeted might be what most sets deep canvassing apart from traditional canvassing. In traditional canvassing, you target your base and the undecided voters. But you skip the houses that have people with opposing views. Why? Because the Fuel-based approach backfires with people who disagree with you. It causes Reactance. With deep canvassing, you *seek out* your opposition. The whole scheme is designed to get people with opposing views to empathize with your cause.

Behavioral science has come up with very few reliable strategies that work for reducing prejudice *in the lab*, and fewer still have extended those findings to the real world. Yet the evidence for deep canvassing is impressive. One recent study monitored the beliefs of Florida voters about a law that protected transgender people from discrimination. Almost 500 voters were interviewed. The researchers found that, on average, exposure to deep canvassing substantially reduces transphobia. How strongly? The shift in support for transgender rights was stronger than the average American shift in gay rights from 1998 and 2012. The same researchers compared those results against 49 other experiments that attempted to change voter opinion through traditional canvassing. It turned out that not a single one of these studies proved effective.

Ask Yes Questions

The moral of these stories is that *asking* is a better approach to getting buy-in than *telling* people what to do. Unfortunately, it isn't quite that simple. Not all questions are good ones. Imagine, for example, asking your kids if they want to eat their vegetables, or asking your boss if she would like to give you a raise. See the problem? If you ask your kids if they want to eat their vegetables, they will just say no. How does that help? It doesn't, of course. What this tells us is that we need to ask the *right* questions.

How do you ask questions that lead to yes rather than no? To find out, two researchers went door to door in a small town asking people if they would be willing to put a large billboard in their front yard that said "Drive Carefully." Quite understandably, only 20 percent of those asked were willing to put a big, ugly billboard in their front yard to promote a good cause. Now suppose you had to double or even *triple* the rate of people who said yes to this request? How would you move the needle that much?

The researchers went to another town to try a different approach. They went door-to-door asking people if they would be willing to display a small sticker in their car or home that said, drive safely. As you might imagine, most people agreed to that much smaller request. Then, a week later, they returned with a follow-up request: would they now be willing to put the same ugly "drive carefully" billboard in their yard. Now, an astonishing 76 percent of residents honored the request. What's going on here?

The innovator's faulty instinct is to begin at the point of tension or disagreement. Asking people to put a big, ugly sign in their yard certainly counts as starting at disagreement because it isn't something people are naturally inclined to do. That's a *no question*. But most people are willing to make a smaller commitment, like wearing a sticker in support of a good cause. "Will you wear this sticker?" begins the conversation at a point of agreement rather than disagreement. "Will you wear this sticker?" is a *yes question*.

New innovations and ideas will be more easily accepted if we begin with questions that reveal acceptance and common ground.

Getting people to say yes to small requests, such as giving feedback on a new product or signing a petition, stokes self-persuasion because it makes them feel more involved in the process. By the time they get the big request, they already identify with the idea.

Let's apply the "*ask yes questions*" approach to an important problem in the restaurant industry – no-shows. No-shows are people who don't cancel their unused restaurant reservations. No-shows are a big problem. Particularly for high-end, low-volume restaurants, just one or two canceled tables can mean the difference between profit and loss.

Picture yourself as a restaurant owner. What might you do to reduce no-show rates? You could punish them for breaking their reservation (e.g., charge them a no-show fee), but that might turn customers off. In his classic book *Influence,* Bob Cialdini tells the story of one restaurant group that used self-persuasion to solve this problem. When you call to make a reservation by phone (this was in the 1990s), there is a conventional script. At the end of the conversation, the reservation taker politely requests that you "please call to cancel if you cannot make it." The restaurant, in essence, is making a demand. They are *telling* you what to do.

One restaurant made a seemingly slight (an ingenious) modification to the script. Rather than tell people to cancel, they asked a *yes question*. They ended the conversation by asking: "If you can't make it, will you call to cancel?" Unless you have Oppositional Defiant Disorder, your answer to that question will be "yes." That little switch, from telling to asking significantly reduced no-show rates.

In sales, this technique is referred to as the *yes ladder*. It means asking questions that begin with agreement. Even when you are dealing with a fierce opponent, there is almost always common ground. A management consultant we worked with shared this advice: "When you are dealing with someone who disagrees with you, particularly when they have strong feelings, begin the conversation with this question: "Are you open to a different point of view?" People feel strong internal pressure to say yes to that question. And in his experience, getting people to say, "Yes, I'd like to hear your opinion," breaks down Reactance and nudges them toward open-mindedness.

How Brainwashing Works

In case you are wondering, this is also how brainwashing works. The term *brainwashing* was coined during the Korean War. In 1952, Frank Schwable, a colonel in the US Marines, was captured by North Korean forces, making him the highest-ranking officer to be taken prisoner of war.[2]

A year later, Schwable made a public appearance that would shock the American public. He falsely confessed that US forces were using biological weapons (things like anthrax and the plague) on Korean soldiers and civilians. Colonel Schwable was just the beginning. Within a few months, over 5,000 US POWs signed false confessions of committing war crimes against the Korean people. The final insult came when 20 American soldiers refused repatriation after the US had withdrawn from the conflict.

These events terrified the US government. They feared that the Communists had developed a new weapon – thought control. To combat the threat, the CIA developed the MK Ultra program, which used LSD and other mind-altering drugs to test whether brainwashing was possible. To the American public, the notion of mindless agents secretly controlled by sinister forces proved to be an irresistible pop culture concept. Movies like *The Manchurian Candidate, Clockwork Orange, The Bourne Identity*, and even *Zoolander* have employed the plot device.

But how does it work? How were American soldiers so quickly turned into propaganda puppets? Scientists studying the POWs who returned home discovered that brainwashing often started with a seemingly innocent question. US prisoners were asked, "Would you agree that no country is perfect?" They were asked, in other words, a *yes question*, because we would all agree that no country is perfect. And once US soldiers agreed with this obvious truth, they were asked the critical, follow-up question: "If, as you say, no country is perfect, then you must think your country is imperfect. What are some of the ways your government has disappointed you?" This is the first in a series of steps to get US soldiers to *persuade themselves* to renounce their own government. Torture can get people to say anything. But torture won't lead soldiers to internalize those beliefs. For that to happen, the propaganda must come from within.

Not every circumstance lends itself to self-persuasion. Tight time pressure, for example, can make it more difficult to invite people into the process. Or perhaps the decision has come from above, and your job is simply to relay the message and make sure change happens. These are moments likely to produce heavy Reactance. When self-persuasion isn't on the table, consider framing the decision as an experiment or pilot test. An experiment is judged on its results. If it doesn't live up to expectations, the experiment can be altered or abandoned. To reframe an initiative from a command to an experiment, you might say something like: "We are going to *try* a new approach. We will give it a five-week trial run. If it isn't delivering results, we will reevaluate and make changes." By conveying flexibility, the experimentation approach can reduce the heavy resistance that a unilateral decision would produce.

Total Participation

This is a good place to tell you about Harwood Manufactory. Harwood Manufactory made women's clothing. The factory was run

by Alfred Marrow, a young, forward-thinking entrepreneur. Before
a career in business, Marrow earned his PhD in psychology. He
worked under none other than Kurt Lewin. Considered by many to
be the founder of social psychology, Lewin's early theories of behavior
change remain influential today. Marrow wanted to take the ideas
they were developing in the lab and put them to the test in the real
world. For four decades, Marrow used the Harwood plant as a testing
ground for progressive management ideas.[3]

One question that fascinated Marrow was how to get workers to
embrace change. A factory is a wonderful place to explore this question. Factory work is routine. Workers settle into their way of doing
things and are notoriously reluctant to change their approach. But
change is necessary. A manufacturing plant requires constant refine-
ment of process and procedures to stay competitive. What's a line
manager to do? Alfred Marrow designed an experiment to find out.

Executives at the plant spotted a cost-cutting opportunity in
how the clothes were made. But to seize it, the workers would have
to break some habits and learn a new routine. Workers were divided
into two groups. In the "no-participation group," workers were called
into a room and told by management that the factory was adopting a
new work procedure. The manager then explained the new change in
operations in great detail. Once trained in the new technique, workers were then sent back to the job with instructions to put the new
method into practice. Classic command-and-control influence, which
would have been the norm in 1950s manufacturing.

In the "total participation group," management described the
problem to the workers and asked for their cost-cutting solutions.
Management and workers collaborated in selecting the best ideas and
worked together to create new protocols. Interestingly, this group
agreed to more significant procedural changes than those in the
no-participation condition. And because it was collaborative, creating
and implementing the change required significantly more training

and planning compared to the one-hour meeting in the other group. So in many ways, the demands for change were bigger in the total participation group.

The differences in these two approaches to innovation were felt immediately. The no-participation group was the typical picture of employee aversion to change. Complaints about the new procedures emerged immediately. The manager-employee dynamic suffered. Employee morale declined, too. Most importantly, the output of the no-participation group dropped dramatically – to about two-thirds its previous output, and output remained low throughout the one-month observation period.

The total participation group had an altogether different response. There was an initial drop in productivity – as they adapted to the new process – but production not only recovered, it exceeded previous rates. Rather than complain about the changes, employees embraced them. Manager-employee relationships were by all accounts good. When change was forced on them, they reacted against it. When employees were invited into the process, they embraced it.

This early study suggests another path to self-persuasion, an approach we call *co-design*. Too often, the innovator's instinct is to write the script entirely. They identify the problem and determine the best solution. The audience simply must follow the innovator's careful instructions. This approach can be tempting because it keeps everything in the innovator's control. But if we want people to embrace our idea, we need to invite them into the process.

Co-Design

In the world of design, there is a name for the process of collective creation with stakeholders. It's called *co-design*. The foundational principle of co-design is that by inviting your employees, customers, and stakeholders to actively participate in the design of a new idea or initiative, these individuals (and their organizations) will be more inclined to embrace and implement the idea once it is ready. Their resulting sense of inventorship makes them an advocate for, and a steward of, the idea itself. Co-design is a technique practiced by product designers, architects, artists, and strategists alike.

MATTER is a 25,000-square-foot health care technology incubator in downtown Chicago. Founded in 2015, its mission is to support health care entrepreneurship by providing startups with affordable office space, expert mentorship, training, workshops, and connections to the important players in the health care industry. From the outset, MATTER needed to establish itself as an independent, nonprofit organization that was able to deliver value to a variety of "customers" who had *very* different and often competing interests.

Large pharmaceutical and medical technology companies would need to be willing to collaborate openly and fairly with startups. Entrepreneurs would need to feel comfortable building their businesses in close proximity to others in the community who may well be competing for the same attention and resources. Rival universities and research institutes would need to participate harmoniously in the MATTER ecosystem in order to support the creation of new ventures. And perhaps most difficult of all, state and city governments would need to agree on which agency would contribute grants and resources, and who would get the credit if the idea proved successful.

With such a diverse range of personalities and priorities to serve, it would be challenging to design an environment and business model that pleased everyone. The key to the success of MATTER would be getting these individuals and groups to *willingly* change the way they interact with one another. These larger organizations and businesses had been very successful operating autonomously. And now they would be asked to collaborate in ways that were . . . unnatural.

Promises of a brighter future for the health care industry, encouragement from the governor of Illinois and the mayor of Chicago, and data demonstrating the power of entrepreneurship and innovation were not enough to get rivals on board.

To get these diverse groups committed to the vision of MATTER, the founding team turned to co-design. The MATTER team facilitated a series of collaborative workshops in which stakeholders were invited to help design the facility. Participants brainstormed, sketched, and prototyped the various elements of the MATTER experience in ways that suited their individual needs. The process also helped highlight where clear areas of Friction might exist as participants storyboarded and, in some cases even role-played, what interactions in the new facility might feel like.

In the end, not every feature or suggestion that stakeholders made was incorporated into the final "product," but most could see their fingerprints on the design of MATTER when it opened its doors. More importantly, these diverse groups had their voices, ideas, and concerns heard *during* the design process – not after it. This instilled a deeper sense of connection to the mission. When MATTER finally opened, the value proposition did not need to be "sold" to anyone – it was already theirs.

MATTER launched in February 2015 with 30 startup companies and around 20 strategic partners, including the state of Illinois, the city of Chicago, and the majority of the Chicago-area universities, hospitals, and research institutes. Today, MATTER has over 300 startup members and over 60 corporate and strategic partners. Companies supported by MATTER have gone on to raise over $1.75 billion in financing, have created over 5,000 jobs, and have impacted the lives of 300 million patients.

Three Rules for Self-Persuasion

The goal of self-persuasion is to get people to *internalize* the message – to avoid Reactance by moving from imposed-insight to self-insight.[4] We looked at two strategies for removing Reactance from your idea: *ask yes questions* and *co-design*. Here are three additional rules for supercharging self-persuasion.

Rule 1: Self-Persuasion Isn't a Suggestion Box

We often see people take what we call the suggestion box approach to self-persuasion. They announce a new idea or initiative and invite people to share feedback. The "if you have any ideas or suggestions, please send us an email" method fails for a couple of reasons. First, how often do you accept those invitations? Probably not often because the path of least resistance is to ignore the request. A weak invitation to participate is not the same as getting people to participate.

The suggestion box approach also fails because giving people a voice – letting them share their opinions – doesn't meet the criteria for self-persuasion. This is a common misconception. With self-persuasion, the aim isn't just to get people talking. The aim is to guide them toward an intended insight. That's why *yes questions* are essential. Asking people to share their opinions on a survey likely doesn't guide them in the direction you intend. If the participation you invite leads them to reach the wrong conclusions, it will do more harm than good.

Rule 2: Make Commitments Public

Self-persuasion becomes more powerful when the commitment is made publicly. Think back to Coach Lad's commitment cards. He could have had players write down their weekly goals privately. But instead, players shared their goals with their teammates. The public nature of the commitment cards creates accountability. Once you've told a room full of people about your plans and goals, you feel more compelled to follow through. But notice where the pressure comes from. It is internal. Imposed pressure backfires because it amplifies Reactance. Strong internal commitment to change is precisely what you want.

The daily standup meeting is a wonderful example of making commitments public. The daily standup, also referred to as the daily scrum or morning rollcall, is a daily meeting often used by software development teams. Each morning, the team holds a short meeting (no more than 15 minutes), where each team member answers three questions: What did I do yesterday that helped the development team meet our goals? What will I do today to help the development team meet our goals? And, Do I see any impediment that prevents me or the development team from meeting our goals?

The daily standup has several functions. It helps teams coordinate and share information. It breaks down silos and creates a sense of common purpose. But beyond the collaborative benefits, the daily standup helps to create and sustain high levels of commitment to the project. Each day, people are telling their team how they will meet their goals. Much like Coach Lad's players, they are making public commitments. This simple practice of self-persuasion creates greater dedication to the mission.

Rule 3: Make It Meaningful

Finally, self-persuasion is most powerful when participation is meaningful and exceeds people's expectations. In the Harwood experiment, we saw that workers who were deeply involved in idea creation (the total participation condition) embraced change, and those who weren't involved (the no-participation condition) rejected change.

There was a third group in the experiment that we didn't tell you about – the "participation through representation" condition. Like the no-participation group, they were instructed to follow a new procedure. But unlike the no-participation group, they were given some voice in the process. They were told that if they had any concerns or ideas, they could share them with an appointed representative who would pass ideas along to management. This third group, as you might expect, reacted exactly like the no-participation group.

The point is that self-persuasion doesn't lend itself to short cuts or empty gestures. Deep canvassing isn't a gimmick. It isn't a parlor trick to get people talking. It is an incredibly thoughtful process that profoundly engages with voters. Only meaningful participation will break down significant opposition to change.

Overcoming Reactance

Defusing Reactance starts with measuring it. Reactance is strongest when your idea challenges people's strongly held beliefs (think politics or religion), when people feel they are under pressure to change, and when people weren't involved in idea creation. To calculate the degree of Reactance your innovation or change initiative will produce, answer these three questions.

1. *Does my idea threaten core beliefs?* This question determines whether your audience is open-minded to the change you are trying to create. If your idea touches on issues you avoid at the Thanksgiving table (politics, religion, social justice), it's probably a core belief.

2. *Does my approach pressure people to change?* When people feel pressured to change, their instinct is to push back in order to maintain their autonomy. Pressure comes in many forms. Penalties for not changing, time pressure, and a demanding message all are strong Reactance generators.

3. *Was your audience excluded?* Is the idea entirely yours or did your audience play a role in the process?

Reactance-Busting Tactics

The secret to overcoming Reactance is to stop pushing for change. Rather than attempting to persuade others, we should help them to persuade themselves. We call this approach to influence and innovation, self-persuasion. Self-persuasion occurs when the arguments and insights for change come from within. This chapter looked at two ways that you can lead people to persuade themselves: *ask yes questions* and *co-design.*

Ask Yes Questions

1. *Are you asking or telling?* Telling people what to do is a form of pressure. *Asking* removes Reactance.

2. *Are you asking a yes question?* The innovator's faulty instinct is to begin the conversation at the point of tension or disagreement. New innovations and ideas will be more easily accepted if we begin with questions that reveal acceptance and common ground.

3. *Can you create public commitments?* Self-persuasion becomes more powerful when the commitment is made publicly.

Co-Design

1. *Can your audience participate in designing the idea?* The foundational principle of co-design is that by inviting people to participate in the design of a new idea, these individuals become more inclined to embrace and implement the idea once it is ready.

2. *Is participation meaningful?* Self-persuasion doesn't lend itself to short cuts or empty gestures. Co-design is most powerful when participation is meaningful and exceeds people's expectations.

11 ⬍ ⬗ ◇ ⬡

Three Case Studies

Putting Friction Theory into Practice

In the following case studies, we apply Friction theory to three real-world scenarios. These situations are complex, and in each there is no one clear solution. This is by design. In each case, we analyze the Frictions as we see them (maybe you'll spot things that we missed) and look at the tactics the innovator used to overcome resistance to change. In some of the cases, the lens of Friction theory has been applied to identify new opportunities for innovation. In others it has been applied to evaluate the presence and magnitude of the headwinds awaiting a given innovation in the market.

We have noted our observations for each case in worksheets we call *Friction Reports*. We use Friction Reports to help diagnose and forecast the impact the Four Frictions have (or will have) on innovation and change initiatives. Friction Reports are designed to be completed collaboratively among colleagues and teammates. The primary objective in completing one of these worksheets is not the report itself, but rather the discussion and debate that it helps facilitate among collaborators. We find them to be an incredibly useful way to note our hypotheses about the Frictions at play as well as their relative magnitude. We hope seeing Friction Theory applied in these different scenarios will empower you to begin to perform similar analysis on your own innovation and change initiatives.

And speaking of which, Friction Reports (as well as many other worksheets, tools, and content developed to help you apply the principles of Friction Theory) may be viewed and downloaded at https://www.humanelementbook.com.

Case Study 1: Dubai's Transition from Oil to Entrepreneurship

For decades, the United Arab Emirates of Dubai had been reliant on oil production to generate a large portion of its national income. By 1990, oil revenue contributed 24 percent of Dubai's GDP and the Emirates was the third largest economy in the Middle East. But just a decade later, things had changed dramatically. Dubai's offshore oil wells began to dry up and petroleum production started to sag. Dubai's role in the petroleum industry radically shifted from being a net exporter of oil to a net *importer*. The natural resource that once contributed almost a quarter of the Emirates' total revenue would contribute less than 1 percent of it by the year 2020. To maintain its prominent standing in the region and the world, Dubai would need to find new engines for economic growth.

In response to these changing conditions, Dubai's leaders decided that it was time to foster a new source of economic growth to ensure its future prosperity – startups. Dubai would rapidly evolve to become a hub of innovation and entrepreneurial activity in the region. But in order to be successful, a lot would need to change.

The Dubai Future Foundation

In 2016, the Dubai government formed the Dubai Future Foundation (DFF). The DFF's mission wasn't just to turn Dubai into a hub for entrepreneurship and innovation. It was more ambitious than that. The government wanted the innovation to come from within. Rather than simply lure established entrepreneurs from abroad to set up shop in Dubai, the government wanted to turn the young citizens of Dubai into successful entrepreneurs. According to Abdulaziz AlJaziri, deputy CEO and chief operations officer of the Dubai Future Foundation, it was not just startup companies that Dubai was hoping to develop: "Even more important than building new ventures was developing entrepreneurial mindsets amongst our younger citizens and residents." AlJaziri and the DFF believed that while entrepreneurial thinking (scanning the market for unmet needs and quickly solving them with new offers) would most certainly sprout startups, it would also empower a generation of young Emiratis to think more creatively about problem-solving overall. This was a mentality he and the country's leaders felt was essential to the success of Dubai's future economy.

With the support of the broader Dubai government, the DFF quickly got to work launching several initiatives designed to inspire young Emiratis to embrace careers in entrepreneurship. There is a playbook countries follow when trying to turn their city or country into an innovation hub. Dubai used this blueprint to create a startup movement of their own.

Programs were created to educate young Emiratis on emerging technology topics such as coding, digital manufacturing, and applied R&D.

- Beautiful new co-working spaces and innovation facilities were built around the city to inspire, attract, and incubate fledgling technologies and startups.

- "Accelerator" programs were launched to provide new ventures with access to funding and mentorship from industry experts inside and outside of Dubai.

- Marketing campaigns were launched to capture national attention and inspire young Emiratis to become entrepreneurs.

Dubai was primed and ready to welcome a flood of new startups – but instead, what they received was a trickle. Despite the excitement generated by the vision of a vibrant startup economy, the beautiful new facilities, mentorship programs, and the coding courses, few young Emiratis felt comfortable taking the entrepreneurial leap. After conducting in-depth interviews with students and studying dozens of career journeys of young Emiratis, some clear insights about the source of the entrepreneurial resistance began to emerge:

Inertia. When the program launched, the idea of becoming an entrepreneur was a foreign concept. Unlike university students in the United States, students in Dubai did not historically have ambitions of creating startups and becoming their own bosses at the age of 21. Whereas the allure of Silicon Valley culture, professional autonomy, and rapid wealth creation inspires college students throughout the US to invent new products in their dorm rooms, Emirati students aspired to something more familiar. At the time, the sought-after job out of school was to be of civil service by holding a position in government. Pursuing a career in entrepreneurship, in other words, is a big shift from the status quo, which would suggest strong Inertia. On the other hand, university students are not firmly rooted in their professional views, and over the course of a four-year program there is time and opportunity to acclimate them to the idea.

Effort. At the time of the DFF's creation, the process for starting a business in Dubai was complicated, time consuming, and expensive. Based on the World Bank ranking of business formation ease referenced in Chapter 5, Dubai ranked 31 on the list. From the moment a young entrepreneur came up with a compelling startup idea to the time they were able to launch, a commercial enterprise could take 12 months or more. The high cost of business formation – which could run upward of $100,000 in registrations and fees – compounded the problem.

Perhaps the biggest Effort-related challenge was ambiguity. The process of business formation was confusing, especially for first-time founders, and navigating the complexities of securing a business license and a commercial bank account was a major deterrent for even the most entrepreneurially minded. And because there wasn't a strong tradition of startups to draw upon, students couldn't readily find mentors to show them the path.

Emotion. The conventional wisdom on startup success suggests that 90 percent of new ventures will fail in their first year or two of life. In San Francisco, a failed startup is seen as a badge of honor. The experience an entrepreneur gains, regardless of the outcome, is believed to provide valuable lessons that can be applied to the next startup a founder chooses to pursue. In Dubai, business failure means something very different. A failed venture might not only bring embarrassment to the entrepreneur, it may also be felt by the entrepreneur's family.

This fear of failure was a major obstacle to change. Why would the parent of a university student want their child to focus her attention on a startup that is likely to fail when she could pursue more traditional studies? Wouldn't that hurt, not help, her future prospects? What might the choice of supporting their child's pursuit of a startup say about them as parents? The stigma surrounding failure was a major impediment to persuading Dubai students to pursue an entrepreneurial path.

Reactance. Young Emiratis were enticed and encouraged to consider a career in entrepreneurship. But there (wisely) wasn't a government mandate to choose that path. Because they weren't pushed to change, the potential for Reactance in this situation seems low.

Overcoming the Frictions

In 2018, the DFF launched an initiative called the *University Entrepreneurship Programme*. It had one purpose: to design a more Frictionless journey for university students wishing to start new business ventures. The program focused on the two biggest Frictions standing in their way.

It was clear from the Effort analysis that if the DFF wanted to spark a wave of young startups to take root in Dubai, additional structural and organizational changes would be necessary. One feature of a healthy startup culture is that entrepreneurs move fast and iterate quickly. To support such a culture, the government would need to redesign the business formation process to accommodate this need for speed.

FRICTION REPORT
Dubai Entrepreneurship

The Idea:
Inspiring young Emeritis to become entrepreneurs

Intended Audience:
Emeriti university students

Inertia

Strength: [L] [M] [✔]

- ☐ Does the idea represent a break from the status quo?
- ☐ Have people had time to acclimate to the idea?
- ☐ Does the proposed change happen gradually or in one big step?

The idea of becoming an entrepreneur was a foreign concept. Emirati students dreamed of holding a service position in the government, not becoming an entrepreneur. Pursuing a career in entrepreneurship is a big shift from the status quo.

The approach did not pressure people to change nor did it exclude the intended audience suggesting a low presence of Reactance.

- ☐ Does the approach pressure people to change?
- ☐ Was the audience excluded from the idea generation and planning process?

Reactance

Strength: [✔] [M] [H]

Effort

Strength: [L] [M] [✔]

- ☐ How much physical and mental exertion is required to implement the change?
- ☐ Do people know how to implement the desired change or is the path ambiguous?

The process of starting a business in Dubai was ambiguous, time consuming, and expensive. Each carry a high degree of Effort on their own, but when combined the Friction can become paralyzing.

The low success rate of most startups and stigma of entrepreneurial failure was very likely to create fear and anxiety for students — but even more so for their parents (who had strong influence over their children's education choices).

- ☐ To what extent might the audience feel threatened by or anxious about the proposed change?
- ☐ Does the idea have the potential to undermine people's broader needs?

Emotion

Strength: [L] [M] [✔]

Free Zones. In May 2019, the government established what were called "Free Economic and Creative Zones" on the campuses of Dubai universities. These Free Zones established universities as innovation enclaves that could play by different rules than the rest of Dubai. In Free Zones, students could establish new business entities and obtain operating licenses within days at significantly discounted fees. Student entrepreneurs also gained easy access to industry experts that could advise the founders on business formation matters such as law, accounting, and IT – all services essential to getting startups up and running and would have been elusive (and most likely unaffordable) to nascent ventures prior to the establishment of the University Entrepreneurship Programme.

Startup grants. The program also provided access to startup grants and seed-funding for first-time entrepreneurs of up to 100,000 AED to offset the cost of salaries and to provide the working capital that young founders need to start a business independent of their parents' financial support.

Roadmap. Finally, a seven-step development roadmap was created to help students navigate their business-building journey. At each stage of development, from inception to launch, the student would be aware of exactly what resources (financial, operational, and community) were available to them and how to access each. This removed ambiguity from the venture formation process for first-time founders.

Overcoming the Fear of Failure

One of the biggest challenges was overcoming the fear of failure. In order to shift the national sentiment around entrepreneurship, some of the stigma of a failed business would need to be removed – both for the students and, perhaps even more importantly, their parents. According to Abdulaziz AlJaziri, "They needed to feel comfortable with the idea that their kids were building companies while in school and not solely focused on their studies," he said. "This was a big shift from the norm. We were honestly not as concerned about inspiring students to want to build startups – at the time there was plenty of excitement around that idea. What we needed to do was remove anxiety from the minds of their parents and their communities."

A clear signal needed to be sent to Emeriti families that stressed the important role university entrepreneurship would play in Dubai's future while being careful not to create Reactance in the process. In January 2019, His Highness Sheikh Mohammed bin Rashid Al Maktoum, prime minister of the UAE and ruler of Dubai, included university-level entrepreneurship as one of nine key strategic goals essential to the future of Dubai in a document called "The Fifty-Year Charter." The charter, which was published on the 50th anniversary of bin Rashid's assuming his first official post in the country, looks out 50 years into the future and frames the most important near-term foundational steps Dubai must take to ensure a vibrant future for decades to come. He called on young Emirati's to play a part in realizing this vision – and when His Highness calls, people listen. From this point on, it was clear that university entrepreneurship was, in essence, a national calling – just like other civil service jobs that university students aspired to.

To inspire new thinking in parents whose children wished to become entrepreneurs, the Dubai government deployed a cutting-edge technology: A thank-you note. Once students progressed their startup idea through the seven-step development roadmap, their parents would receive a letter in the mail, signed by His Highness Sheikh Mohammed bin Rashid Al Maktoum, personally expressing his appreciation for the efforts of their student-entrepreneur.

A crucial nuance of this overture is that the thank-you letter would arrive regardless of the venture's outcome. It was the *attempt* to become an entrepreneur that was being applauded – not the result. The pride parents felt from receiving such an accolade was immeasurable, and soon word of this recognition spread, inspiring more parents to support their children's entrepreneurial calling in support of the country's future.

The Outcome

The University Entrepreneurship Programme was launched in October 2019 with a pilot cohort of 6 local universities. In its first year it doubled the number of participating universities to 12. By 2020, the program had helped launch 308 new student-founded ventures and had quadrupled the number of strategic partner organizations participating in it. Seven new ventures born in the first year's cohort went on to receive innovation grants in the amount of 110,000 AED and were fully operating businesses upon their founders' graduation.

The logistics of creating a startup has gotten easier, too. By 2019, Dubai ranked 11th on the World Bank Ease of Doing

Business list, up 20 places from when the Dubai government began its efforts.

Perhaps most important of all, the national mindset around student entrepreneurship has also begun to change. While a startup in 2016 was viewed as an undesirable career path, today it has evolved in the national consciousness to become a highly aspirational career and is continuing to grow in popularity at universities across Dubai.

Case Study 2: The Rapid Road to Marijuana Legalization

Marijuana was banned in the United States in the 1930s. For 70 years, advocates of legal marijuana tried to change public opinion and the law, with little to show for their efforts. Fueled by economic and social justice concerns, there has always been a strong case for legalization. Here are just a few arguments for legalization: Prohibition has failed to significantly reduce marijuana use, while wasting billions of taxpayer dollars on enforcement. Marijuana prohibition creates social injustice. Black and white Americans use marijuana at similar rates, but black people are roughly four times more likely to be arrested than white Americans for marijuana possession. Prohibition creates a black market that helps organized crime. The Rand Corporation estimates that 30 percent of drug cartel revenue comes from marijuana sales. Legalization, on the other hand, keeps people out of the criminal justice system and raises much-needed tax revenue for state and local governments.

But the American public wasn't listening. As late as the
1990s, the notion of legalization seemed like a libertarian fan-
tasy. Only 24 percent of Americans supported legalization and
no mainstream politician would endorse the cause. Consider the
tremendous Friction operating against change:

Inertia. Going from prohibition to legalization represents a
radical change. To move from harsh penalties for possession
to recreational use is as extreme a change as it gets. The idea
of marijuana legalization was literally a foreign concept. The
only examples of legalization came from a few European
countries with profoundly different policies and values.

Effort. For the voter, it is simply a matter of voting yes or no
to a legalization initiative. For a politician, the ambiguity of
how you regulate a once-illicit drug might be a strong Friction against change.

Emotion. Many voters and politicians feared the consequences
of legalization. Would it lead to higher crime, more road
fatalities, or youth addiction? This fear is particularly acute
for the politician. What if you endorse an initiative that
increases accidents and crime? Even if you believe that outcome is unlikely, it is still a (career) risk.

Reactance. Drug use is a core issue for many people. Using
drugs goes against many people's values, identity, and religious beliefs. The government making a once-taboo drug
suddenly legal might create the perception that marijuana is
being *pushed* onto people who don't want it in their lives. If
that feeling were to take hold, it would almost certainly lead
to fierce protests against legalization efforts.

FRICTION REPORT

Marijuana Legalization

The Idea:
The legalization of marijuana

Intended Audience:
Lawmakers and voters

Inertia

Strength: ✔

☐ Does the idea break from the status quo?

☐ Have people had time to acclimate to the idea?

☐ Does the proposed change happen gradually or in one big step?

Going from prohibition to legalization represents a radical change. To move from harsh penalties for possession to recreational use is as extreme a change as it gets.

Effort

Strength: ✔

☐ How much physical and mental exertion is required to implement the change?

☐ Do people know how to implement the desired change or is the path ambiguous?

For the voter, it is simply a matter of voting "yes" or "no" to a legalization initiative. For a politician, the ambiguity of how you regulate a once illicit drug might be a strong Friction against change.

Drug use is a core issue for many people. Using drugs goes against many people's values, identity, and religious beliefs. If the perception is that marijuana is being pushed onto people, the risk for Reactance is high.

☐ Does the approach pressure people to change?

☐ Was the audience excluded from the idea generation and planning process?

Reactance

Strength: ✔

Many voters and politicians feared the consequences of legalization. Would it lead to higher crime, more road fatalities, or lead to youth addiction?

☐ To what extent might the audience feel threatened by or anxious about the proposed change?

☐ Does the idea have the potential to undermine people's broader needs?

Emotion

Strength: ✔

Overcoming the Frictions

How did the country move from the *war on drugs* to a climate where marijuana legalization enjoys broad support in
Middle America? A big part of the answer is medical marijuana. Rather than push for the full legalization of marijuana,
marijuana advocates changed tactics. They began with a much
smaller policy innovation – tightly controlled marijuana for
cancer patients. This small step is much less radical than full
legalization. When people seek big change, often the only
way to get there is to *start small*. Small steps allow people to
acclimate to the idea, which slowly builds people's comfort
and familiarity with the proposal. Medical marijuana also
reduced Inertia by making the user more familiar. Cancer
affects everyone, particularly adults and the elderly. It meant
that medical marijuana users weren't high school kids and
hippies but professionals – people voters could identify with.
People knew relatives and friends who were medical users.
This served to make the concept of marijuana use less taboo
and more familiar.

Getting people to buy in to medical marijuana is also
a powerful form of self-persuasion. The public overwhelmingly favored medical marijuana for serious illnesses. Getting them to endorse this proposal is a "yes" question. Once
people acclimated to the idea of medical marijuana for
debilitating medical conditions, the next step was to expand
boundaries of the medical conditions covered. "Should people be able to use marijuana to ease the pain for arthritis?"
This was now a "yes" question for the majority of America.
The next step was decriminalization for recreational use. By

the time recreational use went on the ballot, what had previously been an untenable position was now a "yes" question for most people. And by getting people to endorse these positions, average Americans, and not just pot-enthusiasts, began to identify with the cause. By starting from a position of alignment, people didn't react against change but, rather, supported it.

Medical marijuana and the subsequent decriminalization laws also reduced Emotional Friction, particularly for politicians. People had an opportunity to see that relaxing the law didn't lead to a spike in crime. By the time full legalization was put on the table, many of these fears had receded. Without medical marijuana, we suspect that recreational marijuana would never have happened.

The Outcome

As of the beginning of 2021, marijuana is fully legal for recreational use in 15 US states and approved for medical use in 36 states and territories[1] – meaning the majority of Americans now have at least one form of access. Marijuana has been fully or partially decriminalized in 27 states, and there are bills being considered in Congress to legalize marijuana at a national level, and expunge the criminal records of those convicted under prior laws.

A Gallup poll conducted in October 2020 showed that 68 percent of Americans support the legalization of marijuana – an all-time *high*.[2]

Case Study 3: Evening the Playing Field in Homebuying

After the housing crash of 2012, the residential real estate market in the United States began a historic rally. From 2012 to 2021, single-family home values increased by 43 percent. Steady economic recovery from the recession, combined with a decade of historically low interest and mortgage rates, made home ownership desirable to millions of Americans.

While these strong market conditions benefited some, they did not benefit all. The combination of low interest rates, low unemployment, and rising real estate values resulted in highly competitive residential housing markets in metropolitan areas around the United States. In cities such as Seattle, San Francisco, Boston, Denver, New York, and others, typical homebuyers often found themselves bidding for new homes against buyers with the financial wherewithal to make "all-cash" offers. All-cash buyers (as they are known) were the apex predators of residential real estate, and for buyers that required a mortgage in order to purchase a home, trying to outbid them was almost always a losing proposition. This frustrating reality caused thousands of qualified buyers to give up on their dream of home ownership. That is, until Flyhomes, a fast-growing real estate startup, found a way to even the playing field.

The Fuel-Based Origin of Flyhomes

Flyhomes was founded in 2015 by Stephen Lane and Tushar Garg, both MBA students who spent most of their time at business school examining industries they felt might be ripe for disruption. Their research led them to residential real estate.

The homebuying technology companies that existed at the time, like Zillow and Redfin, concentrated on two customer benefits: displaying available new home inventory online for buyers to browse, and offering discount brokerage services that provided buyers with a small amount of cash back on a new home purchase. Lane and Garg believed there was more that could be done to serve the needs of homebuyers. So the duo obtained their real estate licenses and set out to build a different kind of brokerage.

Their first attempt was to offer homebuyers a novel form of incentive for purchasing a house with Flyhomes. Instead of leveraging the discount brokerage model of providing a cash rebate, the two decided to offer their buyers airline miles. They knew that young professionals valued travel and adventure. Why not offer homebuyers one frequent-flyer mile for every dollar they spend on a new house, just as they might earn on buying a meal or a cup of coffee? Buy a $500,000 home and get 500,000 airline miles! They took this idea to several US airlines and quickly signed up both Alaska Airlines and Jet Blue as partners.

Tushar Garg, Flyhomes' CEO, recalls the day that he was sure this approach to home selling was going to be a winner. "I remember that one day Jet Blue sent an email to all of its frequent flyers telling them about the Flyhomes partnership. As soon as that email went out, Flyhomes sign-ups went through the roof – I'm talking thousands of new registrations in a single day. I looked at the number of new users and thought, this is it! Flyhomes is going to be massive!"

It was clear that the travel perks idea had some appeal. At this point, it was just a function of converting those that registered on the website into purchasers. But the conversions

never came. Despite the thousands of new customer registrations on the website, almost none of them bought a home
through Flyhomes. "Our incentives brought them to the
platform but they did not choose to buy a home with us," said
Garg. "Something else was going on."

Accidental Ethnographers

Garg and Lane needed to find a viable new business model,
and quickly. The company had used up almost all of its operating capital pursuing the airline miles strategy. If it was going
to survive long enough to discover a new path, the founders
needed to find a way to keep the fledgling startup afloat.

With real estate broker licenses in hand, Lane and Garg
figured that if they could sell a few homes the old-fashioned
way, perhaps they might learn some valuable insights about
where their points-based business model fell short. More
importantly, they might make enough money to keep the
business running. At the time, Tushar Garg was spending
the semester in his adopted hometown of Seattle where,
prior to business school, he worked at Microsoft. He hoped
that by (literally) loitering outside of a few open houses,
he could convince some homebuyers to work with him as
their agent.

His efforts eventually paid off. Garg was able to leverage
his Microsoft credibility and entrepreneurial hustle to recruit
a few clients, and he immediately got to work trying to help
them buy homes. The experience of working on behalf of
buyers in the hot Seattle real estate market was revelatory. It
quickly became clear to both him and Steve Lane that while
the promise of travel and adventure was appealing to younger
homebuyers, the rewards did absolutely nothing to help them

with their real struggle at the time: successfully acquiring a new home in a highly competitive environment.

"In order to have truly disruptive impact," Garg said, "we were going to need to take the business in a different direction and focus not on perks, but on finding new ways to help customers actually buy the homes they wanted."

The Frictions

What became clear from Steve and Tushar's ethnographic research was that there were powerful Frictions present on both sides of the transaction:

For Sellers:

Emotion. Most homebuyers are unable to afford the purchase of a new home unless they are able to sell their current home first – freeing up the necessary cash to close the deal (often 10–20 percent of the new home purchase price). As a result, many homebuyers are forced to make what are called "home sale contingent offers" to sellers in order get a deal done. Contingent offers are only valid if the buyer is able to sell their current home during a specified time frame.

Effort. If a contingent buyer is unsuccessful in selling their existing home, the offer is void, and sellers must start the listing process all over. Adding insult to injury, their home would now be designated in the market as a "relisted property." Relisted homes carry a stigma. When a buyer sees a house return to the market after being under contract with another buyer, the general assumption is that something must be wrong with the house. Overcoming

FRICTION REPORT

Flyhomes

Inertia   Strength: ☑ M H

☐ Does the idea break from the status quo?

☐ Have people had time to acclimate to the idea?

☐ Does the proposed change happen gradually or in one big step?

Home ownership is not a radical new idea. Furthermore, the transition toward the decision to buy a new home typically happens gradually over months, if not years.

Effort   Strength: C M ☑

☐ How much physical and mental exertion is required to implement the change?

☐ Do people know how to implement the desired change or is the path ambiguous?

The homebuying process is particularly effortful for the buyer. There is a great deal of energy spent on finding a new home, making a competitive offer, then quickly shifting to the work of selling their existing home. There is also the time and expense required to secure a mortgage and successfully close the transaction before a contingency expires.

The process becomes effortful for sellers if a deal falls through and the listing process must begin all over.

The homebuying process does not overtly pressure people to change nor does it exclude the intended audience.

The homebuying process creates a great deal of anxiety for both buyers and sellers.

For buyers the anxiety centers around losing the home they desire if they are unable to compete with all-cash offers or are unable to sell their existing home.

For sellers the anxiety and fear are rooted in the uncertainty of a successful and timely closing.

☐ Does the approach pressure people to change?

☐ Was the audience excluded from the idea generation and planning process?

☐ To what extent might the audience feel threatened by or anxious about the proposed change?

☐ Does the idea have the potential to undermine people's broader needs?

Reactance   Strength: ☑ M H

Emotion   Strength: L M ☑

this stigma can be a challenge, and often relisted houses will end up being sold at a discount over the previous purchase price simply to get a deal done within the timeline sellers require.

For Buyers:

Emotion. Contingent offers are usually time bound – meaning that once an offer is accepted, buyers are in a race against the clock to sell their existing home – a recipe for fear and anxiety. Adding further anxiety is the likely possibility that their existing home may very well be purchased by a buyer who *themselves* may need to make a contingent offer. In a cruel Shakespearean twist, this places the buyer in exactly the same uneasy position as the seller of the home they desire.

Effort. In order to sell their current home, buyers must keep it in "showplace" condition (while simultaneously living in it day-to-day with kids and pets). They must be ready to vacate at a moment's notice for showings and open houses, and they must do all of this while knowing that the purchase of their next home is hanging in the balance. The only way for a buyer to avoid the complexity and stress of entering into a contingent purchase is to make an offer in which they "waive" the home sale contingency entirely. This, too, is precarious for a buyer. By waiving their contingency buyers run the danger of possibly owning two homes at the same time – which is an unaffordable reality for most. Furthermore, many lenders are hesitant to approve new home financing for buyers who may find themselves under the financial strain of owning two homes.

This makes a mortgage for new home purchases both challenging to secure and expensive to obtain due to the added cost of the mortgage insurance most lenders will require buyers to purchase to account for their risk.

Pivoting from Points to Progress

In order to help typical homebuyers compete in competitive markets, Lane and Garg decided to abandon the perks-based business model and focus their attention instead on removing the most significant Frictions acting against both buyers and sellers. They realized that the key was to find a way to provide each party with *certainty*.

Sellers want certainty that an offer will close successfully and in a timely manner. The reason that all-cash buyers were at the top of the real estate food chain was because they were perceived by sellers to be the lowest risk. All-cash buyers did not need to wait for bank financing to be finalized in order to close a deal (which in some markets could take several months and ran the risk of falling through). *Buyers* wanted certainty that they would be able to sell their existing home for a fair price and in a reasonable time frame.

Overcoming the Frictions

To address both buy-side and sell-side Frictions, Flyhomes created an offer called "Trade Up." The program would provide homebuyers with three novel benefits:

A guarantee of sale. Flyhomes would provide buyers with a guaranteed sale of their current home. The company would agree on a purchase price with clients up front, which would give buyers peace of mind that, at minimum, they could count on that money for the purchase of their new home. If Flyhomes was unable to sell their clients' existing home in 90 days, the company would buy the home themselves.

Making all buyers *all-cash* buyers. Flyhomes would also commit to underwrite – in cash – their clients' new home purchase offers. This would essentially make every Flyhomes offer an *all-cash* offer to sellers. This translated to sellers having comfort in the certainty of a successful and timely close.

Adding a listing service. As part of the Trade Up program, Flyhomes would take care of inspecting, deep cleaning, and staging their clients' existing homes. Better still, Flyhomes would wait to list the home until after their client moved out so that they did not have to worry about keeping it clean or quickly disappearing for showings and open houses.

The Outcome

After running the numbers and testing the viability of their idea in the market, the Flyhomes founders were convinced that this approach to homebuying would completely change the game. The company raised a $120 million line of credit to support this new business model and got to work.

The model worked. As of the end of 2020, Flyhomes had closed $2.1 billion worth of sales and transacted close to 3,000 homes. And it turns out, removing Friction for sellers has additional benefits for buyers. In more than 50 percent of successful transactions, Flyhomes bids were *not* the highest purchase price offered. Sellers, as it turns out, value certainty of close more than they value purchase price. In fact, on average,

Flyhomes buyers save 2.4 percent on the purchase price of the homes they buy when compared with buyers working with traditional agents (an amount that averages out to about $18,000 per transaction).

As for the downside risk of the business model: only seven times in the history of the company has Flyhomes needed to take possession of a guaranteed home themselves. Of those few situations, the company has only lost money on a deal twice.

NOTES

Chapter 1: The Law of Attraction

1. Crossman, Edward (1915). How rifle bullets fly. *Scientific American* 113 (1): 24–29.

Chapter 2: Thinking in Fuel

1. Wall Howard, P. (2018). Cadillac salesman sets record for sales, but not without a fight. *USA Today* (February 23). https://www.usatoday.com/story/money/cars/2018/02/23/cadillac-salesman-sets-record-sales-but-not-without-fight/351454002/.
2. Kotler, P. (1967). *Marketing Management: Analysis, Planning and Control.* Englewood Cliffs, NJ: Prentice-Hall.
3. Legg, A. M., and Sweeny, K. (2014). Do you want the good news or the bad news first? The nature and consequences of news order preferences. *Personality and Social Psychology Bulletin* 40 (3): 279–288.
4. Gottman, J., and Silver, J. (1999). *The Seven Principles for Making Marriage Work: A Practical Guide from the Country's Foremost Relationship Expert.* New York: Three Rivers Press.
5. Felps, W., Mitchell, T. R., and Byington, E. (2006). How, when, and why bad apples spoil the barrel: Negative group members and dysfunctional groups. *Research in Organizational Behavior* 27: 175–222.
6. Frijda, N. H. (1988). The laws of emotion. *American Psychologist* 43 (5): 349–358.
7. Gneezy, U., and Rustichini, A. (2000). Pay enough or don't pay at all. *The Quarterly Journal of Economics* 115 (3): 791–810.

8. Aos, S., Phipps, P., Barnoski, R., and Leib, R. (2001). *The Comparative Costs and Benefits of Programs to Reduce Crime.* Document no. 01-05-1201. Olympia: Washington State Institute for Public Policy.
9. This is a story told to us by someone who worked as a recruiter for the US Army.

Chapter 3: Inertia

1. Moreland, R. L., and Beach, S. R. (1992). Exposure effects in the classroom: The development of affinity among students. *Journal of Experimental Social Psychology* 28 (3): 255–276.
2. Zajonc, R. B. (1968). Attitudinal effects of mere exposure. *Journal of Personality & Social Psychology Monograph Supplements* 9 (2, Pt. 2): 1–27.
3. de Lazari-Radek, K., and Singer, P. (2014). *The Point of View of the Universe: Sidgwick and Contemporary Ethics.* OUP Oxford (May 22), p. 25.
4. De Brigard, Felipe (2010). If you like it, does it matter if it's real? *Philosophical Psychology* 23 (1): 43–57.
5. Hiraki, T., Ito, A., and Kuroki, F. (2003). Investor familiarity and home bias: Japanese evidence. *Asia-Pacific Finan Markets* 10: 281–300.

Chapter 4: Overcoming Inertia

1. Hasher, Lynn, Goldstein, D., and Toppino, T. (1977). Frequency and the conference of referential validity. *Journal of Verbal Learning and Verbal Behavior* 16: 107–112. https://web.archive.org/web/20160515062305/http:/www.psych.utoronto.ca/users/hasher/PDF/Frequency%20and%20the%20conference%20Hasher%20et%20al%201977.pdf.
2. van Baaren, R. B., Holland, R. W., Kawakami, K., and van Knippenberg, A. (2004). Mimicry and prosocial behavior. *Psychological Science* 15 (1): 71–74.

Chapter 5: Effort

1. Elner, R.W., and Hughes, R. N. (1978). Energy maximization in the diet of the shore crab, Carcinus Maenas. *Journal of Animal Ecology* 47 (1): 103–116.
2. Hagura, N., Haggard, P., and Diedrichsen, J. (2017). Perceptual decisions are biased by the cost to act. *eLife* (February).

3. Bhalla, M., and Proffitt, D. R. (1999). Visual-motor recalibration in geographical slant perception. *Journal of Experimental Psychology: Human Perception and Performance* 25 (4): 1076–1096.

4. Dixon, M., Freeman, K., and Toman, N. (2010). Stop trying to delight your customers. *Harvard Business Review* (July–August).

5. Maas, J., de Ridder, D. T., de Vet, E., and de Wit, J. B. (2012). Do distant foods decrease intake? The effect of food accessibility on consumption. *Psychology & Health* 27 Suppl 2: 59–73.

Chapter 6: Overcoming Effort

1. Koehler, D. J., White, R. J., and John, L. K. (2011). Good intentions, optimistic self-predictions, and missed opportunities. *Social Psychological and Personality Science* 2 (1): 90–96.

Chapter 7: Emotion

1. Horowitz, D. (1986). The birth of a salesman: Ernest Dichter and the objects of desire, available as an unpublished paper from Hagley Museum, https://www.hagley.org/sites/default/files/HOROWITZ_DICHTER.pdf; Stern, B. B. (2004). The importance of being Ernest: Commemorating Dichter's contribution to advertising research. *Journal of Advertising Research* 44 (2) (June): 165–169.

2. Page, E. (1991). Ernest Dichter, 84, a consultant on consumer motivation, is dead. obituary, *New York Times* (November 23).

3. Williams, R. J. (1957). Is it true what they say about motivation research? *Journal of Marketing* 22 (October): 125–133.

4. Shapiro, Laura (2005). *Something from the Oven: Reinventing Dinner in 1950s America.* New York: Penguin Books, pp. 45, 63–64, 75–77.

5. Case, C. R., and Maner, J. K. (2014). *Journal of Personality and Social Psychology* 107: 1033–1050.

6. Douglass, E. (2005). Full-serve lingers in self-serve world. *Los Angeles Times* (October 9).

Chapter 8: Overcoming Emotion

1. Potchen, E. J. (2006). Measuring observer performance in chest radiology: Some experiences. *Journal of the American College of Radiology* 3 (6): 423–432.

2. Drew, T., Võ, M. L., and Wolfe, J. M. (2013). The invisible gorilla strikes again: Sustained inattentional blindness in expert observers. *Psychol Sci.* 24 (9): 1848–1853. doi:10.1177/0956797613479386.

3. Ohno, Taiichi (1988). *Toyota Production System: Beyond Large-Scale Production.* Portland, OR: Productivity Press. ISBN 0-915299-14-3.

4. Blum, Andrew (2020). How one human-centered insight led to $4 billion in growth for American Express. *IDEO Journal* (December 17).

5. Sydell, Laura (2015). At 90 she's designing tech for aging boomers. National Public Radio, All Tech Considered (January 19).

Chapter 9: Reactance

1. Houser, C. (2020). In fights over face masks, echoes of the American seatbelt wars. *New York Times,* October 15, 2020. https://www.nytimes.com/2020/10/15/us/seatbelt-laws-history-masks-covid.html.

2. Weiss, J. M. (1968). Effects of coping responses on stress. *Journal of Comparative and Physiological Psychology* 65 (2): 251–260.

3. Bown, N. J., Read, D., and Summers, B. (2003). The lure of choice. *Journal of Behavioral Decision Making* 16: 297–308.

4. Pennebaker, J. W., and Sanders, D. Y. (1976). American graffiti: Effects of authority and reactance arousal. *Personality and Social Psychology Bulletin* 2: 264–267.

5. Lord, C. G., Ross, L., and Lepper, M. R. (1979). Biased assimilation and attitude polarization: The effects of prior theories on subsequently considered evidence. *Journal of Personality and Social Psychology* 37 (11): 2098–2109.

6. Feiler, D. C., Tost, L. P., and Grant, A. M. (2012). Mixed reasons, missed givings: The costs of blending egoistic and altruistic reasons in donation requests. *Journal of Experimental Social Psychology* 48 (6): 1322–1328. https://doi.org/10.1016/j.jesp.2012.05.014.

7. Zemack-Rugar, Y., Moore, S. G., and Fitzsimons, G. J. (2017). Just do it! Why committed consumers react negatively to assertive ads. *Journal of Consumer Psychology* 27 (3): 287–301.

8. Costa, D. L., and Kahn, M. E. (2013). Energy conservation "nudges" and environmentalist ideology: Evidence from a randomized residential electricity field experiment. *Journal of the European Economic Association* 11: 680–702.

Chapter 10: Overcoming Reactance

1. Brown, A. (2017). Republicans, Democrats have starkly different views on transgender issues. *Pew Research Center* (November 8). https://www.pewresearch. org/fact-tank/2017/11/08/transgender-issues-divide-republicans-and-democrats/.
2. Boissoneault, L. (2017). The true story of brainwashing and how it shaped America. *Smithsonian Magazine* (May 22).
3. Burnes, B. (2007). Kurt Lewin and the Harwood studies: The foundations of OD. *The Journal of Applied Behavioral Science* 43 (2): 213–231.
4. Cialdini, Robert B. (2007). *Influence: The Psychology of Persuasion.*

Chapter 11: Three Case Studies

1. NCSL (2021). State medical marijuana laws. National Conference of State Legislatures (May 17). https://www.ncsl.org/research/health/state-medical-marijuana-laws.aspx.
2. Brenan, M. (2020). Support for legal marijuana inches up to new high of 68%. *Gallup* (November 9). https://news.gallup.com/poll/323582/support-legal-marijuana-inches-new-high.aspx.

ACKNOWLEDGMENTS

Although there are two names on the book, *The Human Element* is the product of a big team of people who have contributed to its development in many ways. We should begin by acknowledging our publisher, Wiley. We could not have done this without your tremendous support. Special thanks goes to our editor, Zachary Schisgal. Zach, we appreciate the patience and support you have shown to us first-time authors. Thank you for supporting our vision, even when it went against your better judgment.

We'd also like recognize the Kellogg School of Management and the broader Kellogg community. Kellogg students and alumni have touched every part of this book. Many of the stories that enrich this work only came about because one of you took the time to share your experience with us. The Kellogg community has been overwhelmingly generous in supporting and promoting the book. Particular recognition should go to the many students and alumni who offered feedback on early versions of the book. We are privileged to work with the very best students in the world. We can't thank you enough.

Friction Theory builds on the work of many scholars. We would like to highlight two important intellectual debts. First, Friction Theory is an extension of Kurt Lewin's pioneering work on behavior change. His ideas around channel factors deeply informed this book. We have also been inspired by the work of Clay Christensen and Bob Moesta, who together pioneered and popularized the theory of jobs-to-be-done. Their writing on emotional value deeply informed our views on its mirror opposite, Emotional Friction.

We would like to thank the many members of the academic community who gave their time and expertise to the book. Adam Grant was incredibly generous in sharing his knowledge. Loran would like to acknowledge Adam Galinsky for supporting his work and career for over 15 years. David would like to pay special recognition to mentors like Bob Moesta and Tom Kelley, who have generously offered their advice, expertise, and enthusiasm during the writing of this book – and far beyond.

We'd also like to acknowledge and thank the individuals whose stories and expertise helped bring the principles in this book to life. This list includes: Abdulaziz AlJaziri, Staci Alonso, Tushar Garg, Simon King, Brandt Miller, Ali Reda, Jenny Schneider, James Stewart, Chuck Surack, Glen Tullman, and the amazing and continually inspiring Barbara Beskind. Thank you all for the generosity of your stories, insights, and experiences. This book would not be the same without your contributions.

We would also like to reserve a heartfelt moment for our shared mentor, Keith Murnighan. Keith gave so much to both of us. We wish we could have shared this book with you.

Thanks as well to the extended team that helped bring *The Human Element* to life. We'd like to recognize the two amazing graphic designers who gave the book a powerful visual language. Jarrod Ryhal helped design many of the frameworks featured in this book, as well as the Friction Report and other downloadable worksheets. Kyle Fletcher is the ridiculously talented designer responsible for creating the book's provocative and beautiful cover art. They were fantastic collaborators, and we are extremely fortunate to have worked with both of them.

Thanks as well to the publicity team at DEY., Rimjhim Dey and Andy DeSio, who have helped us get the word about Friction Theory out into the world. Finally, to the incomparable Ruthie Seagar who supports us in countless ways and has for many years. Thank you, Ruthie, for everything you do.

Our greatest thanks is reserved for our wives, Erin and Allison, who gave invaluable comments on the book and offered constant advice and support along the way. Recognition goes to Loran Sr., who provided invaluable copy edits and feedback on early versions. And to David's kids, Annie and Teddy, who were kind enough to give him the space to work during the writing process . . . well . . . most of the time. It's wonderful to share the final product of this adventure with all of you.

ABOUT THE AUTHORS

David Schonthal

David Schonthal is an award-winning professor of Innovation & Entrepreneurship at the Kellogg School of Management, where he teaches courses on new venture creation, design thinking, health care innovation, and creativity. In addition to his teaching, he also serves as the faculty director of Kellogg's *Zell Fellows Program*, a selective venture accelerator program designed to help student entrepreneurs successfully launch or acquire new businesses.

Outside of Kellogg, David has been a practitioner of entrepreneurship, design, and innovation for over 20 years. He has spent a decade working at world-renowned design firm *IDEO*, and currently serves as an Operating Partner at *7Wire Ventures*, a health care technology-focused venture capital firm. David is a Global Advisor at *Design for Ventures* (D4V), a Tokyo-based early-stage venture capital fund that invests in design-led Japanese startups, and is the co-founder of *MATTER*, a 25,000-square-foot innovation center in downtown Chicago focused on catalyzing and supporting health care entrepreneurship.

David lives just outside of Chicago with his wife, Erin, and kids, Annie and Teddy. As much as David would like to think he's one-of-a-kind. . .he's actually a triplet.

Loran Nordgren

Loran Nordgren is a professor at the Kellogg School of Management. Loran is one-part behavioral scientist, one-part lecturer, and one-part practitioner. As a behavioral scientist, his research explores the psychological forces that propel and prevent the adoption of new ideas and actions. His research has been published in leading journals such as *Science,* and is regularly discussed in prominent forums such as the *Harvard Business Review.* In recognition of his work, Professor Nordgren has received the Theoretical Innovation Award in experimental psychology.

Loran teaches *Leading Organizational Change.* Its mission is to teach people how to create change in their organizations. A former Fulbright scholar, he has twice received Kellogg's Management *Teacher of the Year* award. As a practitioner, Loran has worked with companies throughout the world on a wide range of behavior change problems, a process he calls Behavioral Design (see Lorannordgren .com for details). Fun Fact: Loran has a giant pet tortoise named Icarus that he hopes will be an intergenerational pet.

INDEX